Meeting SEN
in the Curriculum:
HISTORY

Richard Harris and Ian Luff

 David Fulton Publishers

David Fulton Publishers Ltd
The Chiswick Centre, 414 Chiswick High Road, London W4 5TF

www.fultonpublishers.co.uk

First published in Great Britain in 2004 by David Fulton Publishers

10 9 8 7 6 5 4 3 2 1

Note: The right of Richard Harris and Ian Luff to be identified as the authors of this work
has been asserted by them in accordance with the Copyright, Designs and Patents Act 1988.

Copyright © Richard Harris and Ian Luff 2004

British Library Cataloguing in Publication Data
A catalogue record for this book is available from the British Library.

David Fulton Publishers is a division of Granada Learning, part of ITV plc.

ISBN 1 84312 163 8

Typeset by Servis Filmsetting Ltd, Manchester
Printed and bound in Great Britain by Ashford Colour Press

Meeting SEN
in the Curriculum:
HISTORY

Other titles in the Meeting Special Needs in the Curriculum Series:

Meeting Special Needs in English
Tim Hurst
1 84312 157 3

Meeting Special Needs in Maths
Brian Sharp
1 84312 158 1

Meeting Special Needs in Citizenship
Alan Combes
1 84312 169 7

Meeting Special Needs in Religious Education
Dilwyn Hunt
1 84312 167 0

Meeting Special Needs in Modern Foreign Languages
Sally McKeown
1 84312 165 4

Meeting Special Needs in Design and Technology
Louise Davies
1 84312 166 2

Meeting Special Needs in Art
Kim Earle and Gill Curry
1 84312 161 1

Meeting Special Needs in Music
Victoria Jacquiss and Diane Paterson
1 84312 168 9

Meeting Special Needs in ICT
Sally McKeown
1 84312 160 3

Meeting Special Needs in Science
Carol Holden
1 84312 159 X

Meeting Special Needs in PE and Sport
Crispin Andrews
1 84312 164 6

Meeting Special Needs in Geography
Diane Swift
1 84312 162 X

To Catherine, for her love and support.
RH

To Amanda, James and Anna for their love and understanding.
Also to my Mum, who has always believed in education.
IL

Contents

Contents

Foreword

An entitlement to history is more important than ever. Learning history is about becoming curious, thinking critically, developing moral sensitivity and communicating effectively. Who could claim that, in today's world, any young person should be denied access to a worthwhile history education? A commitment to make the learning of history an enjoyable and challenging experience for each individual pupil lies at the heart of this book. Richard and Ian have provided history teachers with a clear outline of the issues surrounding provision for special educational needs as well as supplying a plethora of ideas that we can use to make learning history a more rewarding experience for everyone.

Thoughtfully and powerfully, Richard and Ian encourage teachers to identify and reflect upon the needs of individual learners. Underpinning their ideas is an absolute refusal to 'dumb down' history in order to make learning inclusive. Instead, they start with the principle that if we think creatively about ways to motivate, challenge and support different pupils, then high-level historical thinking and deep understanding can be brought to all. A central and welcome message is that different pupils do not require radically different things to do. Why should some pupils build a cathedral while others assemble a garden shed? By providing a range of practical strategies for more focused, structured and interactive teaching, this book ensures that the complexity and richness of the past will be experienced by all our pupils.

Richard and Ian's book is based on a careful analysis of their own extensive and excellent classroom practice. They also celebrate and distil some of the best recent teaching and thinking about provision for pupils with special educational needs. Their book is rooted in a deep understanding of the hurdles faced by individual pupils and is based on creative thinking about some of the best strategies to help pupils succeed in studying history. Some of their ideas will reinforce your existing good practice; others will stimulate you to try out new and innovative approaches. Enjoy and learn!

Dr Michael Riley
Senior Lecturer in History Education
Bath Spa University College

Acknowledgements

A number of people have been greatly influential in shaping our careers. In particular, we would like to acknowledge Christine Counsell and Michael Riley, who have been thought provoking and inspirational.

Richard Harris would like to thank his trainees on the PGCE course at Southampton University who have been a great pleasure to work with and have taught him an awful lot. In particular he would like to thank Caroline Lowing for her idea about using slave pictures, which he has used in Chapter 4, and Mark Marande whose lesson on the French Revolution is also mentioned.

Ian Luff acknowledges his debt to George Thomas, Head of Kesgrave whose three-period day has made him look anew at the process of teaching and learning. He would also particularly like to thank Terry Haydn who encouraged him to put pen to paper for his first article.

Contributors to the series

The authors

Richard Harris has been teaching since 1989. He has taught in three comprehensive schools, as history teacher, Head of Department and Head of Faculty. He has also worked as teacher consultant for secondary history in West Berkshire.

Ian Luff is assistant headteacher of Kesgrave High School, Suffolk and has been Head of History in three comprehensive schools.

A dedicated team of SEN specialists and subject specialists have contributed to the *Meeting Special Needs in the Curriculum* series.

Series editor

Alan Combes started teaching in South Yorkshire in 1967 and was Head of English at several secondary schools before taking on the role of Head of PSHE as part of being senior teacher at Pindar School, Scarborough. He took early retirement to focus on his writing career and has authored two citizenship textbooks as well as writing several features for the TES. He has been used as an adviser on citizenship by the DfES and has emphasised citizenship's importance for special needs pupils as a speaker for NASEN.

SEN specialists

Sue Briggs is a freelance education consultant based in Hereford. She writes and speaks on inclusion, special educational needs and disability, and Autistic Spectrum Disorders and is a lay member of the SEN and Disability Tribunal. Until recently, she was SEN Inclusion Co-ordinator for Herefordshire Education Directorate. Originally trained as a secondary music teacher, Sue has extensive experience in mainstream and special schools. For six years she was teacher in charge of a language disorder unit.

Sue Cunningham is a learning support co-ordinator at a large mainstream secondary school in the West Midlands where she manages a large team of learning support teachers and assistants. She has experience of working in both mainstream and special schools and has set up and managed a resource base for pupils with moderate learning difficulties in the mainstream as part of an initiative to promote a more inclusive education for pupils with SEN.

Sally McKeown is an Education Officer with Becta, the government funded agency responsible for managing the National Grid for Learning. She is responsible for the use of IT for learners with disabilities, learning difficulties or additional needs. She is a freelance journalist for the *Times Educational Supplement* and a regular contributor to disability magazines and to *Special Children* magazine. In 2001 her book *Unlocking Potential* was shortlisted for the NASEN Special Needs Book Award.

Subject specialists

English

Tim Hurst has been an SEN co-ordinator in five schools. His current post is at King Edward VI School, Bury St Edmunds, and he started his career at the Willian School in Hertfordshire as an English teacher. Tim later became second in the English department at that school and at about the same time became interested in what was then termed remedial English. Tim has always been committed to the idea of inclusion and the concept of a whole-school approach to special educational needs, particularly after studying for an Advanced Diploma in Special Educational Needs with the Open University. He is especially interested in the role and use of language in teaching.

Maths

Brian Sharp is a Key Stage 3 Mathematics consultant for Herefordshire. Brian has long experience of working both in special and mainstream schools as a teacher of mathematics. He has a range of management experience, including SENCO, mathematics and ICT co-ordinator.

Science

Carol Holden works as a science teacher and assistant SENCO in a mainstream secondary school. She has developed courses for pupils with SEN within science and has gained a graduate diploma and MA in Educational Studies, focusing on SEN.

Modern foreign languages

Sally McKeown is responsible for language-based work in the Inclusion team at Becta. She has a particular interest in learning difficulties and dyslexia. She writes regularly for the *TES*, *Guardian* and *Special Children* magazine.

ICT

Mike North works for ICTC, an independent consultancy specialising in the effective use of ICT in education. He develops educational materials and provides advice and support for the SEN sector.

Sally McKeown is an Education Officer with Becta, the government funded agency responsible for managing the National Grid for Learning and the FERL website. She is responsible for the use of IT for learners with disabilities, learning difficulties or additional needs.

Design and technology

Louise T. Davies is Principal Officer for Design and Technology at the Qualifications and Curriculum Authority and also a freelance consultant. She is an experienced presenter and author of award-winning resources and books for schools. She chairs the Special Needs Advisory Group for the Design and Technology Association.

Religious education

Dilwyn Hunt has worked as a specialist RE adviser, first in Birmingham and now in Dudley. He has a wide range of experience in the teaching of RE, including mainstream and special RE.

Music

Victoria Jaquiss is SEN specialist for music with children with emotional and behavioural difficulties in Leeds. She devised a system of musical notation primarily for use with steel pans, for which, in 2002, she was awarded the fellowship of the Royal Society of Arts.

Diane Paterson works as an inclusive music curriculum teacher in Leeds.

Geography

Diane Swift is a project leader for the Geographical Association. Her interest in special needs developed whilst she was a Staffordshire geography adviser and inspector.

PE and sport

Crispin Andrews is an education/sports writer with nine years' experience of teaching and sports coaching.

Art

Kim Earle is Able Pupils Consultant for St Helens and has been a Head of Art and Design. Kim is also a practising designer jeweller.

Gill Curry is Gifted and Talented Strand Co-ordinator for the Wirral. She has twenty years' experience as Head of Art and has also been an art advisory teacher. She is also a practising artist specialising in print.

Contents of the CD

The CD contains activities and resources that can be amended for individual needs and printed out for use by the purchasing individual or institution. Increasing the font size and spacing will improve accessibility for some students, as will changes in the background colour. Alternatively, print onto pastel-coloured paper for greater ease of reading.

Introduction

All children have the right to a good education and the opportunity to fulfil their potential. All teachers should expect to teach children with special educational needs (SEN) and all schools should play their part in educating children from the local community, whatever their background or ability. (*Removing Barriers to Achievement: The Government's Strategy for SEN, Feb. 2004*)

A raft of legislation and statutory guidance over the past few years has sought to make our mainstream education system more inclusive and ensure that pupils with a diverse range of ability and need are well catered for. This means that all staff need to have an awareness of how children learn and develop in different ways, and an understanding of how barriers to achievement can be removed – or at least minimised.

These barriers often result from inappropriate teaching styles, inaccessible teaching materials or ill-advised grouping of pupils, as much as from an individual child's physical, sensory or cognitive impairments: a fact which is becoming better understood. It is this developing understanding that is now shaping the legislative and advisory landscape of our education system, and making it necessary for all teachers to carefully reconsider their curriculum planning and classroom practice.

The major statutory requirements and non-statutory guidance are summarised in Chapter 1, setting the context for this resource and providing useful starting points for departmental INSET.

It is clear that provision for pupils with special educational needs (SEN) is not the sole responsibility of the Special Educational Needs Co-ordinator (SENCO) and her team of assistants. If, in the past, subject teachers have 'taken a back seat' in the planning and delivery of a suitable curriculum for these children and expected the Learning Support department to bridge the gap between what was on offer in the classroom, and what they actually needed – they can no longer do so. *The Code of Practice, 2002* states:

All teaching and non teaching staff should be involved in the development of the school's SEN policy and be fully aware of the school's procedure for identifying, assessing and making provision for pupils with SEN.

Chapter 2 looks at departmental policy for SEN provision and provides useful audit material for reviewing and developing current practice. The term 'special educational needs' is now widely used and has become something of a catch-all descriptor – rendering it less than useful in many cases. Before the Warnock Report (1978) and subsequent introduction of the term 'special educational needs', any pupils who for whatever reason, (cognitive difficulties, emotional and behavioural difficulties, speech and language disorders) progressed more slowly than the 'norm' were designated 'remedials' and grouped together in the bottom sets, without the benefit, in many cases, of specialist subject teachers.

But the SEN tag was also applied to pupils in special schools who had more significant needs, and who had previously been identified as 'disabled' or even 'uneducable'. Add to these the deaf pupils, those with impaired vision, others with mobility problems, and even children from other countries with a limited understanding of the English language – who may or may not have been highly intelligent – and you have a recipe for confusion, to say the least.

The day-to-day descriptors used in the staffroom are gradually being moderated and refined as greater knowledge and awareness of special needs is built up. (We still hear staff describing pupils as 'totally thick', a 'nutcase' or 'complete moron' – but, hopefully, only as a means of letting off steam!) However, there are terms in common use which, though more measured and well-meaning, can still be unhelpful and misleading. Teachers will describe a child as being 'dyslexic' when they mean that he is poor at reading and writing; 'ADHD' has become a synonym for badly behaved; and a child who seems to be withdrawn or just eccentric is increasingly described as 'autistic'.

The whole process of applying labels is fraught with danger, but sharing a common vocabulary – and more importantly, a common understanding – can help colleagues to express their concerns about a pupil and address the issues as they appear in the classroom. Often, this is better achieved by identifying the particular areas of difficulty experienced by the pupil rather than by identifying the syndrome. The Code of Practice identifies four main areas of difficulty and these are detailed in Chapter 3 – along with an 'at a glance' guide to a wide range of syndromes and conditions, and guidance on how they might present barriers to learning.

There is no doubt that the number of children with special needs being educated in mainstream schools is growing:

> . . . because of the increased emphasis on the inclusion of children with SEN in mainstream schools the number of these children is increasing, as are the severity and variety of their SEN. Children with a far wider range of learning difficulties and variety of medical conditions, as well as sensory difficulties and physical disabilities, are now attending mainstream classes. The implication of this is that mainstream school teachers need to expand their knowledge and skills with regard to the needs of children with SEN. (Stakes and Hornby 2000:3)

The continuing move to greater inclusion means that all teachers can now expect to teach pupils with varied, and quite significant special educational needs at some time. Even five years ago, it was rare to come across children with Asperger's/ Down's/Tourette's Syndrome, Autistic Spectrum Disorder or significant physical/sensory disabilities in community secondary schools. Now, they are entering mainstream education in growing numbers, and there is a realisation that their 'inclusion' cannot be simply the responsibility of the SENCO and support staff. All staff have to be aware of particular learning needs and able to employ strategies in the classroom that directly address those needs.

Chapter 4 considers a range of issues. It looks at what difficulties pupils face when studying history, and examines different ways in which these difficulties can be tackled. It also looks at a wide variety of teaching and learning styles, as well as discussing the components of an inclusive classroom, and how the physical environment and resources, structure of the lesson and teaching approaches can make a real difference to pupils with special needs.

Chapter 5 examines the importance of the need to consider the classroom environment carefully, and then takes a particular look at ICT and how it can be used effectively in the history classroom to address many of the difficulties some pupils face.

Chapter 6 looks at the way role play and the technique of practical demonstration can make the study of the past accessible, and provides sample activities.

The monitoring of pupils' achievements and progress is a key factor in identifying and meeting their learning needs. Those pupils who make slower progress than their peers are often working just as hard, or even harder, but their efforts can go unrewarded. Chapter 7 looks at the way assessment can be used to help pupils with special needs move forward in showing their level of historical understanding. It particularly discusses what we are trying to assess, how to assess it and what actually constitutes progress in history.

Liasing with the SENCO and support staff is an important part of every teacher's role. The SENCO's status in a secondary school often means that this teacher is part of the leadership team and influential in shaping whole-school policy and practice. Specific duties might include:

- ensuring liaison with parents and other professionals;

- advising and supporting teaching and support staff;

- ensuring that appropriate Individual Education Plans are in place;

- ensuring that relevant background information about individual children with special educational needs is collected, recorded and updated;

- making plans for future support and setting targets for improvement;

- monitoring and reviewing action taken.

The SENCO has invariably undergone training in different aspects of special needs provision and has much to offer colleagues in terms of in-house training and advice about appropriate materials to use with pupils. The SENCO should be a frequent and valuable point of reference for all staff, but is often overlooked in this capacity. The presence of the SENCO at the occasional departmental meeting can be very effective in developing teachers' skills in relation to meeting SEN, making them aware of new initiatives and methodology and sharing information about individual children.

In most schools, however, the SENCO's skills and knowledge are channelled to the chalkface via a team of Teaching or Learning Support Assistants (TAs, LSAs). These assistants can be very able and well-qualified, but very underused in the classroom. Chapter 8 looks at how teachers can manage in-class support in a way that makes the best use of a valuable resource.

Throughout the chapters are examples of pupils with particular needs, and lots of ideas about how these might be addressed. There are opportunities to focus on particular ideas or issues. Overall, we hope that this book gives you the chance to consider more carefully how you approach teaching pupils with special needs, and to explore ways that you can develop your own expertise in helping all pupils.

The revised regulations for SEN provision make it clear that mainstream schools are expected to provide for pupils with a wide diversity of needs, and teaching is evaluated on the extent to which all pupils are engaged and enabled to achieve.

This book has been produced in response to the implications of all of this for secondary subject teachers. It has been written by two subject specialists, with support from colleagues who have expertise within the SEN field, so that the information and guidance given is both subject specific and pedagogically sound. The book and accompanying CD provide a resource that can be used with colleagues:

- to shape departmental policy and practice for special needs provision;

- to enable staff to react with a measured response when inclusion issues arise;

- to ensure that every pupil achieves appropriately in history.

CHAPTER 1

Meeting Special Educational Needs – Your Responsibility

Inclusion in education involves the process of increasing the participation of students in, and reducing their exclusion from, the cultures, curricula and communities of local schools. (The Index for Inclusion, 2000)

The Index for Inclusion was distributed to all maintained schools by the Department for Education and Skills and has been a valuable tool for many schools as they have worked to develop their inclusive practice. It supports schools in the review of their policies, practices and procedures, and the development of an inclusive approach, and where it has been used as part of the school improvement process – looking at inclusion in the widest sense – it has been a great success. For many people, however, *The Index* lacked any real teeth, and recent legislation and non-statutory guidance is more authoritative.

The SEN and Disability Act 2001

The SEN and Disability Act 2001 amended the Disability Discrimination Act and created important new duties for schools. Under this Act, schools are obliged:

- to take reasonable steps to ensure that disabled pupils are not placed at a substantial disadvantage in relation to the education and other services they provide. This means they must anticipate where barriers to learning lie and take action to remove them as far as they are able;

- to plan strategically to increase the extent to which disabled pupils can participate in the curriculum, make the physical environment more accessible and ensure that written material is provided in accessible formats.

The reasonable steps taken might include:

- changing policies and practices

- changing course requirements

- changing the physical features of a building

- providing interpreters or other support workers

- delivering courses in alternative ways

- providing materials in other formats

It might, for example, be possible to produce all class materials in electronic form to ensure that they can easily be converted into large print or put into other alternative formats, such as Braille. The staff would then be anticipating 'reasonable adjustments' that might need to be made.

See Appendix 2.1 for an INSET activity and Appendix 2.2 for further detail on SENDA. Appendix 2.3 recommends some strategies that can be employed with pupils with special needs.

The Revised National Curriculum

The Revised National Curriculum (2002) emphasises the provision of effective learning opportunities for all learners, and establishes three principles for promoting inclusion:

- setting suitable learning challenges

- responding to pupils' diverse learning needs

- overcoming potential barriers to learning and assessment

The National Curriculum guidance suggests that staff may need to differentiate tasks and materials, and facilitate access to learning by:

- encouraging pupils to use all available senses and experiences

- planning for participation in all activities

- helping children to manage their behaviour, take part in learning and prepare for work

- helping pupils to manage their emotions

- giving teachers, where necessary, the discretion to teach pupils material from earlier key stages, providing consideration is given to age-appropriate learning contexts. (This means that a fourteen-year-old with significant learning difficulties may be taught relevant aspects of the Programmes of Study (PoS) for history at Key Stage 3 but at the same time might be working on suitable material founded in the PoS for Key Stage 1.)

The Qualifications and Curriculum Authority (QCA) has also introduced performance descriptions (P levels/P scales) to enable teachers to observe and record small steps of progress made by some pupils with SEN. These descriptions outline early learning and attainment for each subject in the National Curriculum, including citizenship, RE and PSHE. They chart progress up to NC level 1 through eight steps. The performance descriptions for P1 to P3 are common across all subjects and outline the types and range of general performance that some pupils with learning difficulties might characteristically demonstrate. From level P4 onwards, many believe it is possible to describe performance in a way that indicates the emergence of subject-focused skills, knowledge and understanding. P levels are described in Chapter 7.

The Code of Practice for Special Educational Needs

The Revised Code of Practice (implemented in 2002) describes a cyclical process of planning, target setting and review for pupils with SEN. It also makes clear the expectation that the vast majority of pupils with special needs will be educated in mainstream settings. Those identified as needing over and above what the school can provide from its own resources, however, are nominated for 'School Action Plus', and outside agencies will be involved in planned intervention. This may involve professionals from the Learning Support Service, a specialist teacher or therapist, or an educational psychologist, working with the school's SENCO to put together an Individual Education Plan (IEP) for the pupil. In a minority of cases (the numbers vary widely between LEAs) pupils may be assessed by a multi-disciplinary team on behalf of the local education authority, whose representatives then decide whether or not to issue a statement of SEN. This is a legally binding document detailing the child's needs and setting out the resources which should be provided. It is reviewed every year.

Fundamental Principles of the Special Needs Code of Practice

- A child with special educational needs should have their needs met.

- The special educational needs of children will normally be met in mainstream schools or settings.

- The views of the child should be sought and taken into account.

- Parents have a vital role to play in supporting their child's education.

- Children with special educational needs should be offered full access to a broad, balanced and relevant education, including an appropriate curriculum for the Foundation stage and the National Curriculum.

Ofsted

Ofsted inspectors are required to make judgements about a school's inclusion policy, and how this is translated into practice in individual classrooms. According to Ofsted (2003) the following key factors help schools to become more inclusive:

- a climate of acceptance of all pupils

- careful preparation of placements for SEN pupils

- availability of sufficient suitable teaching and personal support

- widespread awareness among staff of the particular needs of SEN pupils and an understanding of the practical ways of meeting these needs in the classroom

- sensitive allocation to teaching groups and careful curriculum modification, timetables and social arrangements

- availability of appropriate materials and teaching aids and adapted accommodation

- an active approach to personal and social development, as well as to learning

- well-defined and consistently applied approaches to managing difficult behaviour

- assessment, recording and reporting procedures which can embrace and express adequately the progress of pupils with more complex SEN who make only small gains in learning and PSD

- involving parents/carers as fully as possible in decision-making, keeping them well informed about their child's progress and giving them as much practical support as possible

- developing and taking advantage of training opportunities, including links with special schools and other schools

Policy into practice

Effective teaching for pupils with special educational needs is, by and large, effective for all pupils, but as schools become more inclusive, teachers need to be able to respond to a wider range of needs. The Government's strategy for SEN (*Removing Barriers to Learning*, 2004) sets out ambitious proposals to 'help teachers expand their repertoire of inclusive skills and strategies and plan confidently to include children with increasingly complex needs'.

In many cases, pupils' individual needs will be met through greater differentiation of tasks and materials, i.e. school-based intervention as set out in the SEN Code of Practice. A smaller number of pupils may need access to specialist equipment and approaches or to alternative or adapted activities, as part of a School Action Plus programme, augmented by advice and support from external specialists. The QCA, on its website 2003, encourages teachers to take specific action to provide access to learning for pupils with special educational needs by:

(a) providing for pupils who need help with communication, language and literacy, through:

- using texts that pupils can read and understand
- using visual and written materials in different formats, including large print, symbol text and Braille
- using ICT, other technological aids and taped materials
- using alternative and augmentative communication, including signs and symbols
- using translators, communicators and amanuenses

(b) planning, where necessary, to develop pupils' understanding through the use of all available senses and experiences by:

- using materials and resources that pupils can access through sight, touch, sound, taste or smell
- using word descriptions and other stimuli to make up for a lack of first-hand experiences
- using ICT, visual and other materials to increase pupils' knowledge of the wider world
- encouraging pupils to take part in everyday activities such as play, drama, class visits and exploring the environment

(c) planning for pupils' full participation in learning and in physical and practical activities by:

- using specialist aids and equipment
- providing support from adults or peers when needed
- adapting tasks or environments
- providing alternative activities, where necessary

(d) helping pupils to manage their behaviour, to take part in learning effectively and safely, and, at Key Stage 4, to prepare for work by:

- setting realistic demands and stating them explicitly
- using positive behaviour management, including a clear structure of rewards and sanctions
- giving pupils every chance and encouragement to develop the skills they need to work well with a partner or a group
- teaching pupils to value and respect the contribution of others
- encouraging and teaching independent working skills
- teaching essential safety rules

(e) helping individuals to manage their emotions, particularly trauma or stress, and to take part in learning by:

- identifying aspects of learning in which the pupil will engage and plan short-term, easily achievable goals in selected activities
- providing positive feedback to reinforce and encourage learning and build self-esteem
- selecting tasks and materials sensitively to avoid unnecessary stress for the pupil
- creating a supportive learning environment in which the pupil feels safe and is able to engage with learning
- allowing time for the pupil to engage with learning and gradually increasing the range of activities and demands

Pupils with disabilities

The QCA goes on to provide guidance on pupils with disabilities, pointing out that not all pupils with disabilities will necessarily have special educational needs. Many learn alongside their peers with little need for additional resources beyond the aids which they use as part of their daily life, such as a wheelchair, a hearing aid or equipment to aid vision. Teachers' planning must ensure, however, that these pupils are enabled to participate as fully and effectively as possible in the curriculum by:

- planning appropriate amounts of time to allow for the satisfactory completion of tasks. This might involve:
  - taking account of the very slow pace at which some pupils will be able to record work, either manually or with specialist equipment, and of the physical effort required
  - being aware of the high levels of concentration necessary for some pupils when following or interpreting text or graphics, particularly when using vision aids or tactile methods, and of the tiredness which may result
  - allocating sufficient time, opportunity and access to equipment for pupils to gain information through experimental work and detailed observation, including the use of microscopes
  - being aware of the effort required by some pupils to follow oral work, whether through use of residual hearing, lip reading or a signer, and of the tiredness or loss of concentration which may occur
- planning opportunities, where necessary, for the development of skills in practical aspects of the curriculum. This might involve:
  - providing alternative or adapted activities in history for pupils who are unable to use available ICT
  - ensuring that all pupils can be included and participate safely in history field work, local studies and visits to museums, historic buildings and sites

- identifying aspects of Programmes of Study and attainment targets that may present specific difficulties for individuals. This might involve:
  - helping visually impaired pupils to access maps and visual resources in history
  - providing opportunities for pupils to develop strength in depth where they cannot meet the particular requirements of a subject,
  - discounting these aspects in appropriate individual cases when required to make a judgement against level descriptions

Disapplying pupils

This is a distinct possibility for pupils now, but what would be the consequences of denying pupils access to a history education? Counsell (2003) tells the tale of Melanie. She was studying twentieth-century dictators. She had been well taught, but in a class test she was faced with the simple question, 'name a dictator'. She thought long and hard, and eventually wrote the answer 'Mutlin'! Mutlin, the hybrid dictator, a bit of Mussolini, Hitler and Stalin all rolled into one. Should Melanie be disapplied from history because she cannot master this small detail, or should she be encouraged and helped to understand the past more carefully? If she were to stop studying history because it is difficult, then what chance has she of making sense of the world in which she lives? How can she make sensible decisions about participation in a democratic society?

Education is not simply about finding out what you are no good at and then giving it up, but about helping pupils understand things they don't understand in the first place! History is not just about facts, it provides children with an insight into society, how it operates, how it has been shaped and come into existence, what values permeate society. History is about human thought, intention and action. To deny pupils access to such a subject is to deny them access to an understanding of the world in which they live. Yes, for some pupils history is difficult, but it is important that we find ways that allow them to have access to the richness of this subject.

Summary

Pupils with a wide range of needs – physical/sensory, emotional, cognitive and social – are present in increasing numbers, in all mainstream settings. Government policies point the way, with inclusion at the forefront of national policy – but it is up to teachers to make the rhetoric a reality. Teachers are ultimately responsible for all the children they teach. In terms of participation, achievement and enjoyment – the buck stops here!

CHAPTER 2

Departmental Policy

It is crucial that departmental policy describes a strategy for meeting pupils' special educational needs within the particular curricular area. The policy should set the scene for any visitor to the history department – from supply staff to inspectors – and make a valuable contribution to the departmental handbook. The process of developing a department SEN policy offers the opportunity to clarify and evaluate current thinking and practice within the history team and to establish a consistent approach.

The policy should:

- clarify the responsibilities of all staff and identify any with specialist training and/or knowledge;

- describe the curriculum on offer and how it can be differentiated;

- outline arrangements for assessment and reporting;

- guide staff on how to work effectively with support staff;

- identify staff training.

The starting point will be the school's SEN policy as required by the Education Act 1996, with each subject department 'fleshing out' the detail in a way which describes how things work in practice. The writing of a policy should be much more than a paper exercise completed to satisfy the senior management team and Ofsted inspectors: it is an opportunity for staff to come together as a team and create a framework for teaching history in a way that makes it accessible to all pupils in the school.

Where to start when writing a policy

An audit can act as a starting point for reviewing current policy on SEN or it can inform the writing of a new policy. It will involve gathering information and reviewing current practice with regard to pupils with SEN, and is best completed by the whole of the department, preferably with some additional advice from the SENCO or another member of staff with responsibility for SEN within the school. An audit carried out by the whole department can provide a valuable opportunity for professional development if it is seen as an exercise in sharing good practice and encouraging joint planning. But before embarking on an audit, it is worth investing some time in a department meeting or training day, to raise awareness of special educational needs legislation and to establish a shared philosophy. Appendix 2 contains OHT layouts and an activity to use with staff. (These are also on the accompanying CD, with additional exercises you may choose to use.)

The following headings may be useful in establishing a working policy:

General statement

- What does legislation and DfES guidance say?
- What does the school policy state?
- What do members of the department have to do to comply with it?

Definition of SEN

- What does SEN mean?
- What are the areas of need and the categories used in the Code of Practice?
- Are there any special implications within the subject area?

Provision for staff within the department

- How is information shared?
- Who has responsibility for SEN within the department?
- How and when is information shared?
- Where and what information is stored?

Provision for pupils with SEN

- How are pupils with SEN assessed and monitored in the department?
- How are contributions to IEPs and reviews made?
- What criteria are used for organising teaching groups?
- What alternative courses are offered to pupils with SEN?
- What special internal and external examination arrangements are made?
- What guidance is available for working with support staff?

Resources and learning materials

- Is there any specialist equipment used in the department?

- How are resources developed?

- Where are resources stored?

Staff qualifications and Continuing Professional Development needs

- What qualifications do the members of the department have?

- What training has taken place?

- How is training planned?

- Is a record kept of training completed and training needs?

Monitoring and reviewing the policy

- How will the policy be monitored?

- When will the policy be reviewed?

The content of a SEN departmental policy

This section gives detailed information on what a SEN policy might include. Each heading is expanded with some detailed information and raises the main issues with regard to teaching pupils with SEN. At the end of each section there is an example statement. The example statements can be personalised and brought together to make a policy. Strategies to use with pupils with various special educational needs are suggested in the examples in this chapter and are gathered as an example policy in Appendix 2.3.

General statement with reference to the school's SEN policy

All schools must have a SEN policy according to the Education Act 1996. This policy will set out basic information on the school's SEN provision, and how the school identifies, assesses and provides for pupils with SEN, including information on staffing and working in partnership with other professionals and parents.

Any department policy needs to have reference to the school SEN policy.

Example

> All members of the department will ensure that the needs of all pupils with SEN are met, according to the aims of the school and its SEN policy.

Definition of SEN

It is useful to insert at least the four areas of SEN in the department policy, as used in the Code of Practice for Special Educational Needs.

TABLE 2.1 THE FOUR AREAS OF SEN			
Cognition and Learning Needs	**Behavioural, Emotional and Social Development Needs**	**Communication and Interaction Needs**	**Sensory and/or Physical Needs**
Specific learning difficulties (SpLD)	Behavioural, emotional and social difficulties (BESD)	Speech, language and communication needs	Hearing impairment (HI)
Dyslexia	Attention Deficit Disorder (ADD)	Autistic Spectrum Disorder (ASD)	Visual impairment (VI)
Moderate learning difficulties (MLD)	Attention Deficit Hyperactivity Disorder (ADHD)	Asperger's Syndrome	Multi-sensory impairment (MSI)
Severe learning difficulties (SLD)			Physical difficulties (PD)
Profound and multiple learning difficulties (PMLD)			OTHER

Provision for staff within the department

In many schools, each department nominates a member of staff to have special responsibility for SEN provision (with or without remuneration). This can be very effective where there is a system of regular liaison between department SEN representatives and the SENCO in the form of meetings or paper communications or a mixture of both.

The responsibilities of this post may include liaison between the department and the SENCO, attending any liaison meetings and providing feedback via meetings and minutes, attending training, maintaining the departmental SEN information and records and representing the needs of pupils with SEN at departmental level. This post can be seen as a valuable development opportunity for staff. The name of this person should be included in the policy.

How members of the department raise concerns about pupils with SEN can be included in this section. Concerns may be raised at specified departmental meetings before referral to the SENCO. An identified member of the department could make referrals to the SENCO and keep a record of this information.

Reference to working with support staff will include a commitment to planning and communication between staff. There may be information on inviting support staff to meetings, resources and lesson plans.

A reference to the centrally held lists of pupils with SEN and other relevant information will also be included in this section. A note about confidentiality of information should be included.

Example

> The member of staff with responsibility for overseeing the provision of SEN within the department will attend liaison meetings and feedback to other members of the department. Other responsibilities will include maintaining the department's SEN information file, attending appropriate training and disseminating this to all departmental staff. All information will be treated with confidentiality.

Provision for pupils with SEN

It is the responsibility of all staff to know which pupils have SEN and to identify any pupils having difficulties. Pupils with SEN may be identified by staff within the department in a variety of ways. These may be listed and could include:

- observation in lessons

- assessment of class work

- homework tasks

- end of module tests

- progress checks

- annual examinations

- reports

Setting out how pupils with SEN are grouped within the history department may include specifying the criteria used and/or the philosophy behind the method of grouping.

Example

The pupils are grouped according to ability as informed by Key Stage 2 results, reading scores and any other relevant performance, social or medical information.

Monitoring arrangements and details of how pupils can move between groups should also be set out. Information collected may include:

- National Curriculum levels
- departmental assessments
- reading scores
- advice from pastoral staff
- discussion with staff in the SEN dept
- information provided on IEPs

Special examination arrangements need to be considered not only at Key Stages 3 and 4 but also for internal examinations. How and when these will be discussed should be clarified. Reference to the SENCO and examination arrangements from the examination board should be taken into account. Ensuring that staff in the department understand the current legislation and guidance from central government is important, so a reference to the SEN Code of Practice and the levels of SEN intervention is helpful within the policy. Here is a good place also to put a statement about the school behaviour policy and rewards and sanctions, and how the department will make any necessary adjustments to meet the needs of pupils with SEN.

Example

It is understood that pupils with SEN may receive additional support if they have a statement of SEN, are at School Action Plus or School Action. The staff in the history department will aim to support the pupils to achieve their targets as specified on their IEPs and will provide feedback for IEP or statement reviews. Pupils with SEN will be included in the departmental monitoring system used for all pupils. Additional support will be requested as appropriate.

Resources and learning materials

The department policy needs to specify what differentiated materials are available, where they are kept and how to find new resources. This section could include a statement about working with support staff to develop resources or access specialist resources as needed, and the use of ICT. Teaching strategies may also be identified if appropriate. Advice on more specialist equipment can be sought as necessary, possibly through LEA support services: contact details may be available from the SENCO, or the department may have direct links. Any specially bought subject text or alternative/appropriate courses can be specified as well as any external assessment and examination courses.

Example

> The department will provide suitably differentiated materials and, where appropriate, specialist resources for pupils with SEN. Additional texts are available for those pupils working below National Curriculum level 3. At Key Stage 4, an alternative course to GCSE is offered at Entry level but, where possible, pupils with SEN will be encouraged to reach their full potential and follow a GCSE course. Support staff will be provided with curriculum information in advance of lessons and will also be involved in lesson planning. A list of resources is available in the department handbook and on the noticeboard.

Staff qualifications and Continuing Professional Development needs

It is important to recognise and record the qualifications and special skills gained by staff within the department. Training can include not only external courses but also in-house INSET and opportunities such as observing other staff, working to produce materials with other staff, and visiting other establishments. Staff may have hidden skills that might enhance the work of the department and the school, for example some staff might be proficient in the use of sign language.

Example

> A record of training undertaken, specialist skills and training required will be kept in the department handbook. Requests for training will be considered in line with the department and school improvement plan.

Monitoring and reviewing the policy

Any policy to be effective needs regular monitoring and review. These can be planned as part of the yearly cycle. The responsibility for the monitoring can rest with the Head of Department, but will have more effect if supported by someone from outside acting as a critical friend. This could be the SENCO or a member of the senior management team in school.

Example

> The department SEN policy will be monitored by the Head of Department on a planned annual basis, with advice being sought from the SENCO as part of a three-yearly review process.

Conclusion

Creating a departmental SEN policy should be a developmental activity to improve the teaching and learning for all pupils but especially for those with special or additional needs. The policy should be a working document that will evolve and change; it is there to challenge current practice and to encourage improvement for both pupils and staff. If departmental staff work together to create the policy, they will have ownership of it; it will have true meaning and be effective in clarifying practice.

(See Appendices and CD for INSET activity material.)

CHAPTER 3

Different Types of SEN

This chapter is a starting point for information on the special educational needs most frequently occurring in the mainstream secondary school. It describes the main characteristics of each learning difficulty, with practical ideas for use in subject areas, and contacts for further information. Some of the tips are based on good secondary practice while others encourage teachers to try new or less familiar approaches.

The special educational needs outlined in this chapter are grouped under the headings used in the SEN Code of Practice (DfES 2001):

- cognition and learning

- behavioural, emotional and social development

- communication and interaction

- sensory and/or physical needs

(See Table 2.1 in Chapter 2.)

The labels used in this chapter are useful when describing pupils' difficulties, but it is important to remember not to use the label in order to define the pupil. Put the pupil before the difficulty, saying 'the pupil with special educational needs' rather than 'the SEN pupil', 'pupils with MLD' rather than 'MLDs'.

Remember to take care in using labels when talking with parents, pupils or other professionals. Unless a pupil has a firm diagnosis, and parents and pupil understand the implications of that diagnosis, it is more appropriate to describe the features of the special educational need rather than use the label, for example a teacher might describe a pupil's spelling difficulties but not use the term 'dyslexic'.

The number and profile of pupils with special educational needs will vary from school to school, so it is important to consider the pupil with SEN as an individual within your school and subject environment. The strategies contained in this chapter will help teachers adapt that environment to meet the needs of individual pupils within the subject context. For example, rather than saying, 'He can't read the worksheet', recognise that the worksheet is too difficult for the pupil, and adapt the work accordingly.

There is a continuum of need within each of the special educational needs listed here. Some pupils will be affected more than others, and show fewer or more of the characteristics described.

The availability and levels of support from professionals within a school (e.g. SENCOs, support teachers, Teaching Assistants) and external professionals (e.g. educational psychologists, Learning Support Service staff, medical staff) will depend on the severity of pupils' SEN. This continuum of need will also impact on the subject teacher's planning and allocation of support staff.

Pupils with other less common special educational needs may be included in some secondary schools, and additional information on these conditions may be found in a variety of sources. These include the school SENCO, LEA support services, educational psychologists and the Internet.

Asperger's Syndrome

Asperger's Syndrome is a disorder at the able end of the autistic spectrum. People with Asperger's Syndrome have average to high intelligence but share the same Triad of Impairments. They often want to make friends but do not understand the complex rules of social interaction. They have impaired fine and gross motor skills, with writing being a particular problem. Boys are more likely to be affected – with the ratio being 10:1 boys to girls. Because they appear 'odd' and naïve, these pupils are particularly vulnerable to bullying.

Main characteristics:

- **Social interaction**
  Pupils with Asperger's Syndrome want friends but have not developed the strategies necessary for making and sustaining friendships. They find it very difficult to learn social norms and to pick up on social cues. Highly social situations, such as lessons, can cause great anxiety.

- **Social communication**
  Pupils have appropriate spoken language but tend to sound formal and pedantic, using little expression and with an unusual tone of voice. They have difficulty using and understanding non-verbal language, such as facial expression, gesture, body language and eye-contact. They have a literal understanding of language and do not grasp implied meanings.

- **Social imagination**
  Pupils with Asperger's Syndrome need structured environments, and to have routines they understand and can anticipate. They excel at learning facts and figures, but have difficulty understanding abstract concepts and in generalising information and skills. They often have all-consuming special interests.

How can the subject teacher help?

- Liaise closely with parents, especially over homework.
- Create as calm a classroom environment as possible.
- Allow the pupil to sit in the same place for each lesson.
- Set up a work buddy system for your lessons.
- Provide additional visual cues in class.
- Give time for the pupil to process questions and respond.
- Make sure pupils understand what to do.
- Allow alternatives to writing for recording.
- Use visual timetables and task activity lists.
- Prepare for changes to routines well in advance.
- Give written homework instructions and stick them into an exercise book.
- Have your own class rules and apply them consistently.

The National Autistic Society, 393, City Road, London EC1V 1NG
Tel: 0845 070 4004 Helpline (10a.m. – 4p.m., Mon–Fri) Tel: 020 7833 2299
Fax: 020 7833 9666
Email: nas@nas.org.uk Website: http://www.nas.org.uk

Attention Deficit Disorder (with or without hyperactivity) (ADD/ ADHD)

Attention Deficit Hyperactivity Disorder is a term used to describe children who exhibit overactive behaviour and impulsivity and who have difficulty in paying attention. It is caused by a form of brain dysfunction of a genetic nature. ADHD can sometimes be controlled effectively by medication. Children of all levels of ability can have ADHD.

Main characteristics:

- difficulty in following instructions and completing tasks
- easily distracted by noise, movement of others, objects attracting attention
- often doesn't listen when spoken to
- fidgets and becomes restless, can't sit still
- interferes with other pupils' work
- can't stop talking, interrupts others, calls out
- runs about when inappropriate
- has difficulty in waiting or taking turns
- acts impulsively without thinking about the consequences

How can the subject teacher help?

- Make eye contact and use the pupil's name when speaking to him.
- Keep instructions simple – the one sentence rule.
- Provide clear routines and rules, and rehearse them regularly.
- Sit the pupil away from obvious distractions, e g. windows, the computer.
- In busy situations direct the pupil by name to visual or practical objects.
- Encourage the pupil to repeat back instructions before starting work.
- Tell the pupil when to begin a task.
- Give two choices – avoid the option of the pupil saying 'No': ' Do you want to write in blue or black pen?'
- Give advanced warning when something is about to happen. Change or finish with a time, e.g. 'In two minutes I need you (pupil name) to . . .'
- Give specific praise – catch him being good, give attention for positive behaviour.
- Give the pupil responsibilities so that others can see him in a positive light and he develops a positive self-image.

ADD Information Services, PO Box 340, Edgware, Middlesex, HA8 9HL
Tel: 020 8906 9068
ADDNET UK Website: www.btinternet.com/~black.ice/addnet/

Autistic Spectrum Disorders (ASD)

The term 'Autistic Spectrum Disorders' is used for a range of disorders affecting the development of social interaction, social communication and social imagination and flexibility of thought. This is known as the 'Triad of Impairments'. Pupils with ASD cover the full range of ability, and the severity of the impairment varies widely. Some pupils also have learning disabilities or other difficulties. Four times as many boys as girls are diagnosed with an ASD.

Main characteristics:

- **Social interaction**
  Pupils with an ASD find it difficult to understand social behaviour and this affects their ability to interact with children and adults. They do not always understand social contexts. They may experience high levels of stress and anxiety in settings that do not meet their needs or when routines are changed. This can lead to inappropriate behaviour.

- **Social communication**
  Understanding and use of non-verbal and verbal communication is impaired. Pupils with an ASD have difficulty understanding the communication of others and in developing effective communication themselves. They have a literal understanding of language. Many are delayed in learning to speak, and some never develop speech at all.

- **Social imagination and flexibility of thought**
  Pupils with an ASD have difficulty in thinking and behaving flexibly which may result in restricted, obsessional, or repetitive activities. They are often more interested in objects than people, and have intense interests in one particular area, such as trains or vacuum cleaners. Pupils work best when they have a routine. Unexpected changes in those routines will cause distress. Some pupils with Autistic Spectrum Disorders have a different perception of sounds, sights, smell, touch, and taste, and this can affect their response to these sensations.

How can the subject teacher help?

- Liaise with parents as they will have many useful strategies.
- Provide visual supports in class: objects, pictures, etc.
- Give a symbolic or written timetable for each day.
- Give advance warning of any changes to usual routines.
- Provide either an individual desk or with a work buddy.
- Avoid using too much eye contact as it can cause distress.
- Give individual instructions, using the pupil's name, e.g. 'Paul, bring me your book.'
- Allow access to computers.
- Develop social interactions using a buddy system or Circle of Friends.
- Avoid using metaphor, idiom or sarcasm – say what you mean in simple language.
- Use special interests to motivate.
- Allow difficult situations to be rehearsed by means of Social Stories.

BEHAVIOURAL, EMOTIONAL, SOCIAL DEVELOPMENT NEEDS

This term includes behavioural, emotional, social difficulties and Attention Deficit Disorder with or without hyperactivity. These difficulties can be seen across the whole ability range and have a continuum of severity. Pupils with special educational needs in this category are those that have persistent difficulties despite an effective school behaviour policy.

Behavioural, emotional, social difficulty (BESD)

Main characteristics:

- inattentive, poor concentration and lack of interest in school/school work

- easily frustrated, anxious about changes

- unable to work in groups

- unable to work independently, constantly seeking help

- confrontational – verbally aggressive towards pupils and/or adults

- physically aggressive towards pupils and/or adults

- destroys property – their own/ others

- appears withdrawn, distressed, unhappy, sulky, may self-harm

- lacks confidence, acts extremely frightened, lacks self-esteem

- finds it difficult to communicate and to accept praise

How can the subject teacher help?

- Check the ability level of the pupil and adapt the level of work to this.

- Consider the pupil's strengths and use them.

- Tell the pupil what you expect in advance, as regards work and behaviour.

- Talk to the pupil to find out a bit about them.

- Set a subject target with a reward system.

- Focus your comments on the behaviour, not on the pupil, and offer an alternative way of behaving when correcting the pupil.

- Use positive language and verbal praise whenever possible.

- Tell the pupil what you want them to do: 'I need you to . . . ,' 'I want you to . . .' rather than ask.

- Give the pupil a choice between two options.

- Stick to what you say.

- Involve the pupil in responsibilities to increase self-esteem and confidence.

- Plan a 'time out' system. Ask a colleague for help with this.

SEBDA is the new name for the Association of Workers for Children with emotional and behavioural difficulties.
Website: www.awcebd.co.uk

Cerebral palsy

Cerebral palsy is a persistent disorder of movement and posture. It is caused by damage or lack of development to part of the brain before or during birth or in early childhood. Problems vary from slight clumsiness to more severe lack of control of movements. Pupils with CP may also have learning difficulties. They may use a wheelchair or other mobility aid.

Main characteristics:

There are three main forms of cerebral palsy:

- *spasticity* – disordered control of movement associated with stiffened muscles

- *athetosis* – frequent involuntary movements

- *ataxia* – an unsteady gait with balance difficulties and poor spatial awareness

  Pupils may also have communication difficulties.

How can the subject teacher help?

- Talk to parents, the physiotherapist – and the pupil.

- Consider the classroom layout.

- Have high academic expectations.

- Use visual supports: objects, pictures, symbols.

- Arrange a work/subject buddy.

- Speak directly to the pupil rather than through a Teaching Assistant.

- Ensure access to appropriate IT equipment for the subject – and that it is used.

Scope, PO Box 833, Milton Keynes, MK12 5NY
Tel: 0808 800 3333 (Freephone helpline) Fax: 01908 321051
Email: cphelpline@scope.org.uk Website: http://www.scope.org.uk

Down's Syndrome (DS)

Down's Syndrome is the most common identifiable cause of learning disability. This is a genetic condition caused by the presence of an extra chromosome 21. People with DS have varying degrees of learning difficulties, ranging from mild to severe. They have a specific learning profile with characteristic strengths and weaknesses. All share certain physical characteristics but will also inherit family traits in physical features and personality. They may have additional sight, hearing, respiratory, and heart problems.

Main characteristics:

- delayed motor skills
- take longer to learn and consolidate new skills
- limited concentration
- difficulties with generalisation, thinking and reasoning
- sequencing difficulties
- stronger visual than aural skills
- better social than academic skills

How can the subject teacher help?

- Ensure that the pupil can see and hear you and other pupils.
- Speak directly to the pupil and reinforce with facial expression, pictures and objects.
- Use simple, familiar language in short sentences.
- Check instructions have been understood.
- Give time for the pupil to process information and formulate a response.
- Break lessons up into a series of shorter, varied, and achievable tasks.
- Accept other ways of recording: drawings, tape/video recordings, symbols, etc.
- Set differentiated tasks linked to the work of the rest of the class.
- Provide age-appropriate resources and activities.
- Allow working in top sets to give good behaviour models.
- Provide a work buddy.
- Expect unsupported work for part of each lesson.

The Down's Association, 155 Mitcham Road, London SW17 9PG
Tel: 0845 230 0372
Email: info@downs-syndrome.org.uk
Website: http://www.downs-syndrome.org.uk

Fragile X Syndrome

Fragile X Syndrome is caused by a malformation of the X chromosome and is the most common form of inherited learning disability. This intellectual disability varies widely, with up to a third having learning problems ranging from moderate to severe. More boys than girls are affected but both may be carriers.

Main characteristics:

- delayed and disordered speech and language development
- difficulties with the social use of language
- articulation and/or fluency difficulties
- verbal skills better developed than reasoning skills
- repetitive or obsessive behaviour such as hand-flapping, chewing, etc.
- clumsiness and fine motor co-ordination problems
- attention deficit and hyperactivity
- easily anxious or overwhelmed in busy environments

How can the subject teacher help?

- Liaise with parents.
- Make sure the pupil knows what is to happen in each lesson – provide visual timetables, work schedules or written lists.
- Ensure the pupil sits at the front of the class, in the same seat for all lessons.
- Arrange a work/subject buddy.
- Where possible, keep to routines and give prior warning of all changes.
- Make instructions clear and simple.
- Use visual supports: objects, pictures, symbols.
- Allow the pupil to use a computer to record and access information.
- Give lots of praise and positive feedback.

Fragile X Society, Rood End House, 6 Stortford Road, Dunmow, CM6 1DA
Tel: 01424 813147 (Helpline) Tel: 01371 875100 (Office)
Email: info@fragilex.org.uk Website:http://www.fragilex.org.uk

Moderate learning difficulties (MLD)

The term 'moderate learning difficulties' is used to describe pupils who find it extremely difficult to achieve expected levels of attainment across the curriculum, even with a differentiated and flexible approach. These pupils do not find learning easy and can suffer from low self-esteem and sometimes exhibit unacceptable behaviour as a way of avoiding failure.

Main characteristics:

- difficulties with reading, writing and comprehension
- unable to understand and retain basic mathematical skills and concepts
- immature social and emotional skills
- limited vocabulary and communication skills
- short attention span
- under-developed co-ordination skills
- lack of logical reasoning
- inability to transfer and apply skills to different situations
- difficulty remembering what has been taught
- difficulty with organising themselves, following a timetable, remembering books and equipment

How can the subject teacher help?

- Check the pupil's strengths, weaknesses and attainment levels.
- Establish a routine within the lesson.
- Keep tasks short and varied.
- Keep listening tasks short or broken up with activities.
- Provide word lists, writing frames, shorten text.
- Try alternative methods of recording information, e.g. drawings, charts, labelling, diagrams, use of ICT.
- Check previously gained knowledge and build on it.
- Repeat information in different ways.
- Show the child what to do or what the expected outcome is, demonstrate or show examples of completed work.
- Use practical, concrete, visual examples to illustrate explanations.
- Question the pupil to check they have grasped a concept or can follow instructions.
- Make sure the pupil always has something to do.
- Use lots of praise, instant rewards – catch them trying hard.

The MLD Alliance, c/o The Elfrida Society, 34 Islington Park Street, London N1 1PX.
Website: www.mldalliance.com/executive.htm

Physical disability (PD)

There is a wide range of physical disabilities, and pupils with PD cover all academic abilities. Some pupils are able to access the curriculum and learn effectively without additional educational provision. They have a disability but do not have a special educational need. For other pupils, the impact on their education may be severe, and the school will need to make adjustments to enable them to access the curriculum.

Some pupils with a physical disability have associated medical conditions which may impact on their mobility. These include cerebral palsy, heart disease, spina bifida and hydrocephalus, and muscular dystrophy. Pupils with physical disabilities may also have sensory impairments, neurological problems, or learning difficulties. They may use a wheelchair and/or additional mobility aids. Some pupils will be mobile but may have significant fine motor difficulties which require support. Others may need augmentative or alternative communication aids.

Pupils with a physical disability may need to miss lessons to attend physiotherapy or medical appointments. They are also likely to become very tired as they expend greater effort to complete everyday tasks. Schools will need to be flexible and sensitive to individual pupil needs.

How can the subject teacher help?

- Get to know pupils and parents and they will help you make the right adjustments.

- Maintain high expectations.

- Consider the classroom layout.

- Allow the pupil to leave lessons a few minutes early to avoid busy corridors and give time to get to next lesson.

- Set homework earlier in the lesson so instructions are not missed.

- Speak directly to the pupil rather than through a Teaching Assistant.

- Let pupils make their own decisions.

- Ensure access to appropriate IT equipment for the lesson – and that it is used!

- Give alternative ways of recording work.

- Plan to cover work missed through medical or physiotherapy appointments.

- Be sensitive to fatigue, especially at the end of the school day.

Semantic Pragmatic Disorder

Semantic Pragmatic Disorder is a communication disorder which falls within the autistic spectrum. 'Semantic' refers to the meanings of words and phrases, and 'pragmatic' refers to the use of language in a social context. Pupils with this disorder have difficulties understanding the meaning of what people say and in using language to communicate effectively. Pupils with SPD find it difficult to extract the central meaning – saliency – of situations.

Main characteristics:

- delayed language development
- fluent speech but may sound stilted or over-formal
- may repeat phrases out of context from videos or adult conversations
- difficulty understanding abstract concepts
- limited or inappropriate use of eye contact, facial expression or gesture
- motor skills problems

How can the subject teacher help?

- Sit the pupil at the front of the room to avoid distractions.
- Use visual supports: objects, pictures, symbols.
- Pair with a work/subject buddy.
- Create a calm working environment with clear classroom rules.
- Be specific and unambiguous when giving instructions.
- Make sure instructions are understood, especially when using subject-specific vocabulary that can have another meaning in a different context.

AFASIC, 2nd Floor, 50–52 Great Sutton Street, London EC1V 0DJ
Tel: 0845 355 5577 (Helpline 11a.m.–2p.m.) Tel: 020 7490 9410 Fax: 020 7251 2834
Email: info@afasic.org.uk Website: http://www.afasic.org.uk

Sensory impairments

Hearing impairment (HI)

The term 'hearing impairment' is a generic term used to describe all hearing loss. The main types of loss are monaural, conductive, sensory and mixed loss. The degree of hearing loss is described as mild, moderate, severe or profound. Some children rely on lip reading, others will use hearing aids, and a small proportion will have British Sign Language (BSL) as their primary means of communication.

How can the subject teacher help?

- Check the degree of loss the pupil has.

- Check the best seating position (e.g. away from the hum of OHP, computers, with good ear to speaker).

- Check that the pupil can see your face for facial expressions and lip reading.

- Provide a list of vocabulary, context and visual clues, especially for new subjects.

- During class discussion allow only one pupil to speak at a time and indicate where the speaker is.

- Check that any aids are working and if there is any other specialist equipment available.

- Make sure the light falls on your face and lips. Do not stand with your back to a window.

- If you use interactive whiteboards, ensure that the beam does not prevent the pupil from seeing your face.

- Ban small talk.

Royal Institute for the Deaf (RNID), 19–23 Featherstone Street, London EC2A 8SL
Tel: 0808 808 0123
British Deaf Association (BDA) 1–3 Worship Street, London ECZA 2AB
British Association of Teachers of the Deaf (BATOD), The Orchard, Leven,
North Humberside, HU17 5QA
Website: www.batod.org.uk

Visual impairment (VI)

Visual impairment refers to a range of difficulties, including those experienced by pupils with monocular vision (vision in one eye), those who are partially sighted and those who are blind. Pupils with visual impairment cover the whole ability range and some pupils may have other SEN.

How can the subject teacher help?

- Check the optimum position for the pupil, e.g. for a monocular pupil their good eye should be towards the action.

- Always provide the pupil with their own copy of the text.

- Provide enlarged print copies of written text.

- Check use of ICT (enlarged icons, talking text, teach keyboard skills).

- Do not stand with your back to the window as this creates a silhouette and makes it harder for the pupil to see you.

- Draw the pupil's attention to displays – which they may not notice.

- Make sure the floor is kept free of clutter.

- Tell the pupil if there is a change to the layout of a space.

- Ask if there is any specialist equipment available (enlarged print dictionaries, lights, talking scales).

Royal National Institute for the Blind (RNIB), 224, Great Portland St, London W1W 5AA
Tel: 020 7388 1266
Website: www.mid.org.uk

Multi-sensory impairment

Pupils with multi-sensory impairment have a combination of visual and hearing difficulties. They may also have other additional disabilities that make their situation complex. A pupil with these difficulties is likely to have a high level of individual support.

How can the subject teacher help?

- The subject teacher will need to liaise with support staff to ascertain the appropriate provision within each subject.

- Consideration will need to be given to alternative means of communication.

- Be prepared to be flexible and to adapt tasks, targets and assessment procedures.

Severe learning difficulties (SLD)

This term covers a wide and varied group of pupils who have significant intellectual or cognitive impairments. Many have communication difficulties and/or sensory impairments in addition to more general cognitive impairments. They may also have difficulties in mobility, co ordination and perception. Some pupils may use signs and symbols to support their communication and understanding. Their attainments may be within or below level 1 of the National Curriculum, or in the upper P scale range (P4–P8), for much of their school careers.

How can the subject teacher help?

- Liaise with parents.
- Arrange a work/subject buddy.
- Use visual supports: objects, pictures, symbols.
- Learn some signs relevant to the subject.
- Allow time for the pupil to process information and formulate responses.
- Set differentiated tasks linked to the work of the rest of the class.
- Set achievable targets for each lesson or module of work.
- Accept different recording methods: drawings, audio or video recordings, photographs, etc.
- Give access to computers where appropriate.
- Give a series of short, varied activities within each lesson.

Profound and multiple learning difficulties (PMLD)

Pupils with profound and multiple learning difficulties have complex learning needs. In addition to very severe learning difficulties, pupils have other significant difficulties, such as physical disabilities, sensory impairments or severe medical conditions. Pupils with PMLD require a high level of adult support, both for their learning needs and for their personal care.

They are able to access the curriculum through sensory experiences and stimulation. Some pupils communicate by gesture, eye pointing or symbols, others by very simple language. Their attainments are likely to remain in the early P scale range (P1–P4) throughout their school careers (that is below level 1 of the National Curriculum). The P scales provide small, achievable steps to monitor progress. Some pupils will make no progress or may even regress because of associated medical conditions. For this group, experiences are as important as attainment.

How can the subject teacher help?

- Liaise with parents and Teaching Assistants.

- Consider the classroom layout.

- Identify possible sensory experiences in your lessons.

- Use additional sensory supports: objects, pictures, fragrances, music, movements, food, etc.

- Take photographs to record experiences and responses.

- Set up a work/subject buddy rota for the class.

- Identify times when the pupil can work with groups.

MENCAP,
117–123, Golden Lane, London EC1Y 0RT
Tel: 020 7454 0454 Website: http://www.mencap.org.uk

SPECIFIC LEARNING DIFFICULTIES (SpLD)

The term 'specific learning difficulties' covers dyslexia, dyscalculia and dyspraxia.

Dyslexia

The term 'dyslexia' is used to describe a learning difficulty associated with words and it can affect a pupil's ability to read, write and/or spell. Research has shown that there is no one definitive definition of dyslexia or one identified cause, and it has a wide range of symptoms. Although found across a whole range of ability levels, the idea that dyslexia presents as a difficulty between expected outcomes and performance is widely held.

Main characteristics:

- The pupil may frequently lose their place when reading, make a lot of errors with the high frequency words, have difficulty reading names, and have difficult blending sounds and segmenting words. Reading requires a great deal of effort and concentration.

- The pupil's work may seem messy with crossing outs, similarly shaped letters may be confused, such as b/d/p/q, m/w, n/u, and letters in words may be jumbled, such as tired/tried. Spelling difficulties often persist into adult life and these pupils become reluctant writers.

How can the subject teacher help?

- Be aware of the type of difficulty and the pupil's strengths.

- Teach and allow the use of word processing, spell checkers and computer-aided learning packages.

- Provide word lists and photocopies of copying from the board.

- Consider alternative recording methods, e.g. pictures, plans, flow charts, mind maps.

- Allow extra time for tasks, including assessments and examinations.

The British Dyslexia Association
Tel: 0118 966 8271 Website: www.bda-dyslexia.org.uk
Dyslexia Institute
Tel: 07184 222 300 Website: www.dyslexia-inst.org.uk

Dyscalculia

The term 'dyscalculia' is used to describe a difficulty in mathematics. This might be either a marked discrepancy between the pupil's developmental level and general ability on measures of specific maths ability, or a total inability to abstract or consider concepts and numbers.

Main characteristics:

- In numeracy, the pupil may have difficulty counting by rote, writing or reading numbers, miss out or reverse numbers, have difficulty with mental maths, and be unable to remember concepts, rules and formulae.

- In maths based concepts, the pupil may have difficulty with money, telling the time, with directions, right and left, with sequencing events or may lose track of turns, e.g. in team games, dance.

How can the subject teacher help?

- Provide number/word/rule/formulae lists and photocopies of copying from the board.
- Make use of ICT and teach the use of calculators.
- Encourage the use of rough paper for working out.
- Plan the setting out of work with it well spaced on the page.
- Provide practical objects that are age appropriate to aid learning.
- Allow extra time for tasks, including assessments and examinations.

Website: www.dyscalculia.co.uk

Dyspraxia

The term 'dyspraxia' is used to describe an immaturity with the way in which the brain processes information, resulting in messages not being properly transmitted.

Main characteristics:

- difficulty in co-ordinating movements, may appear awkward and clumsy
- difficulty with handwriting and drawing, throwing and catching
- difficulty following sequential events, e.g. multiple instructions
- may misinterpret situations, take things literally
- limited social skills resulting in frustration and irritability
- some articulation difficulties

How can the subject teacher help?

- Be sensitive to the pupil's limitations in games and outdoor activities and plan tasks to enable success.
- Ask the pupil questions to check his understanding of instructions/tasks.
- Check seating position to encourage good presentation (both feet resting on the floor, desk at elbow height and ideally with a sloping surface to work on).

Website: www.dyspraxiafoundation.org.uk

Speech, language and communication difficulties (SLCD)

Pupils with speech, language and communication difficulties have problems understanding what others say and/or making others understand what they say. Their development of speech and language skills may be significantly delayed. Speech and language difficulties are very common in young children but most problems are resolved during the primary years. Problems that persist beyond the transfer to secondary school will be more severe. Any problem affecting speech, language and communication will have a significant effect on a pupil's self-esteem, and personal and social relationships. The development of literacy skills is also likely to be affected. Even where pupils learn to decode, they may not understand what they have read. Sign language gives pupils an additional method of communication. Pupils with speech, language and communication difficulties cover the whole range of academic abilities.

Main characteristics:

- **Speech difficulties**
  Pupils who have difficulties with expressive language may experience problems in articulation and the production of speech sounds, or in co-ordinating the muscles that control speech. They may have a stammer or some other form of dysfluency.

- **Language/communication difficulties**
  Pupils with receptive language impairments have difficulty understanding the meaning of what others say. They may use words incorrectly with inappropriate grammatical patterns, have a reduced vocabulary, or find it hard to recall words and express ideas. Some pupils will also have difficulty using and understanding eye-contact, facial expression, gesture and body language.

How can the subject teacher help?

- Talk to parents, speech therapist – and the pupil.
- Learn the most common signs for your subject.
- Use visual supports: objects, pictures, symbols.
- Use the pupil's name when addressing them.
- Give one instruction at a time, using short, simple sentences.
- Give time to respond before repeating a question.
- Make sure pupils understand what they have to do before starting a task.
- Pair with a work/subject buddy.
- Give access to a computer or other IT equipment appropriate to the subject.
- Give written homework instructions.

ICAN 4 Dyer's Buildings, Holborn, London EC1N 2QP
Tel: 0845 225 4071
Email: info@ican.org.uk website: http://www.ican.org.uk
AFASIC 2nd Floor, 50–52, Great Sutton Street, London EC1V 0DJ
Tel: 0845 355 5577 (Helpline) Tel: 020 7490 9410 Fax: 020 7251 2834
Email: info@afasic.org.uk Website: http://www,afasic.org.uk

Tourette's Syndrome (TS)

Tourette's Syndrome is a neurological disorder characterised by tics. Tics are involuntary, rapid or sudden movements or sounds that are frequently repeated. There is a wide range of severity of the condition with some people having no need to seek medical help while others have a socially disabling condition. The tics can be suppressed for a short time but will be more noticeable when the pupil is anxious or excited.

Main characteristics:

Physical tics

Physical tics range from simple blinking or nodding, through more complex movements, to more extreme conditions such as echopraxia (imitating actions seen) or copropraxia (repeatedly making obscene gestures).

Vocal tics

Vocal tics may be as simple as throat clearing or coughing, but can progress to be as extreme as echolalia (the repetition of what was last heard) or coprolalia (the repetition of obscene words).

TS itself causes no behavioural or educational problems but other, associated disorders such as Attention Deficit Hyperactivity Disorder (ADHD) or Obsessive Compulsive Disorder (OCD) may be present.

How can the subject teacher help?

- Establish a rapport with the pupil.

- Talk to the parents.

- Agree an 'escape route' signal should the tics become disruptive.

- Allow pupil to sit at the back of the room to prevent staring.

- Give access to a computer to reduce handwriting.

- Make sure pupil is not teased or bullied.

- Be alert for signs of anxiety or depression.

Tourette Syndrome (UK) Association
PO Box 26149, Dunfermline, KY12 7YU
Tel: 0845 458 1252 (Helpline) Tel: 01383 629600 (Admin)
Fax: 01383 629609
Email: enquiries@tsa.org.uk Website: http://www.tsa.org.uk

CHAPTER 4

Teaching and Learning

When considering teaching pupils with special needs, many teachers automatically think of differentiation in terms of the creation of worksheets aimed at pupils of differing abilities. Though this has a place within the history classroom, much can be achieved at a more generic level by considering how teachers approach teaching within the class as a whole.

The key word is access. Pupils can achieve as long as they can get into the work on the 'ground floor'. The idea that lower ability pupils cannot deal with too much information often results in teachers offering a slimmed-down curriculum and expecting pupils to understand complex issues on the basis of less information – quite often they need more information to make something intelligible. The result can be pupils at the bottom end of the ability range either being made to feel inferior in some way as they get the 'easy' worksheet, or unable to do the work because they don't have enough knowledge to make sense of something. In such a scenario, pupils can too easily become disengaged and disenchanted. We need to motivate pupils and make them feel valued, build up their confidence and self-esteem.

Part of the problem has been the perception that history is too difficult a subject for pupils with special needs. On one level, history is reliant on language skills because of the predominance of writing and reading required within the subject. At another level, history requires a lot of abstract thought, trying to grapple with complex ideas set in a time that is beyond the comprehension of many pupils. This raises unique problems for the history teacher.

This section addresses many of these issues. Teaching is a complex business when it comes to disentangling its essence to convey it to someone else. Much of what follows, therefore, is overlapping, but for the sake of clarity, the issues need to be discussed separately.

Language

It is clear that the teacher needs to find ways to help pupils access the language necessary to study the history curriculum.

Subject-specific language

Subject-specific vocabulary can create problems. History is full of problematic words and phrases. Consider the word 'church'. To most pupils, a church is a building. To talk, therefore, about the power of the Church in the Middle Ages, becomes a baffling statement – how can a building have power!? Words such as 'party', 'state' and 'power' are likely to mean different things to different pupils, yet the exact use of this terminology is important in communicating ideas clearly in history. Pupils need to be taught explicitly, within context, what these words mean, and what is associated with these meanings. By starting with what pupils understand by the terms, new meanings can be added that are context specific. The use of a 'slippery word' board can be valuable here. Identifying words within a lesson, and asking pupils to determine in what sense they are being used, will test and extend their proficiency in technical vocabulary. New words can be added as they are encountered, creating a more dynamic word bank that pupils have some control over. Such a technique can be used to highlight words that may mean different things in different contexts, or be used for difficult, abstract words.

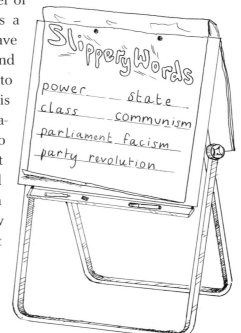

INSET Activity

As a history department:

1. Think about when in your teaching the words on the slippery word board will be encountered.

2. How might these words confuse pupils?

3. How do their meanings alter depending on the context in which they are used?

4. When and how will they be explained in the classroom?

5. Look at your areas of study: what other words might you include on a 'slippery word' board?

Using symbols

Where pupils need access to alternative communication, the use of symbols is an excellent method of support which is well established in special schools but not in mainstream. The use of such visual prompts and reinforcements can actually be useful with a wide range of pupils.

Tina and Mike Detheridge in *Literacy Through Symbols* describe how a study of the Vikings was made accessible to pupils with significant communication difficulties by the availability of a set of symbols. Pupils were able to use the computer, some with the help of an overlay keyboard, to produce their own written material to include in their booklets on the Vikings. The pupils enjoyed being able to read from their booklets in a group, and in order to include a pupil who had no speech, some phrases about the Vikings were programmed into a communication device. 'His response indicated that he was pleased to be able to join in with the other pupils' (Martin and Gummett 2001:87).

The   Vikings   came   to   Britain   in   their   longships.

The illustration above shows writing which uses a symbol for each word. Others may choose to symbolise only the key words.

A project reported by the Curriculum Council for Wales (1991) explored ways in which the history curriculum could be made more accessible to pupils with learning difficulties. Although carried out some time ago, this project was one of the first in which teachers started to use symbols to enhance curriculum access, and still gives a good illustration of how pupils can access new concepts. In this project, the pupils were provided with symbols of several artefacts used in the Victorian era. They were asked to identify the items and suggest what they were used for. This activity prompted an animated discussion between the pupils. They were then asked to identify the comparable item used today. Various games were devised such as snap – between modern and Victorian pairs, or grouping items by category from the same era.

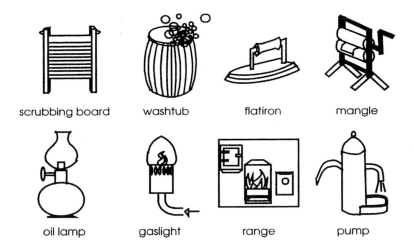

A large cross-section of a Victorian house and of a modern one were also drawn and the items were placed in the appropriate rooms in the house of the associated period. This exercise showed that the pupils had grasped many of the differences between today and the Victorian era, for example, 'the iron went in the living room because it was heated on the range' (Curriculum Council for Wales 1991:27)

Pupil talk

Talking is important in the classroom, as the work of Vygotsky and Bruner shows. By discussing ideas, pupils can exchange views and learn from each other. In addition, we need to consider where the pupils are starting from in the lesson, as they come to the lessons with their own preconceptions about the past. These views are likely to be personal and fragmented. They may be 'instinctive reactions' along the lines of 'I think people in the past were stupid', or may have been informed by such things as media images, books, and adverts. Whatever the source of information, we, as history teachers, need to start with the pupils' own views and understanding. By understanding their preconceptions and misconceptions, pupils of all abilities can be moved forward. This also provides a concrete point from which to build and with which pupils are familiar. As McAleavy 1994: 164 explains:

> The difference between everyday exemplification and work on historical content is simply that weaker pupils feel comfortable with their knowledge of their own world, whereas they are often baffled and disorientated by the unusual terms and names of periods in the past.

The value of this approach is that it allows the pupils to feel confident, starting with the known. It also gives a chance for initial ideas to be shaped and modified as views conflict with those of others.

A trainee teacher started work on the 'Black Peoples of the Americas' unit by asking pupils to draw a picture of a slave. This was done simply and quickly, before the pupils were given the chance to compare ideas. The examples in Figure 4.1 were drawn by pupils in a bottom set Year 9 class. They all show

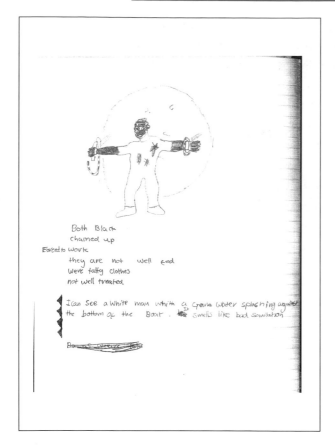

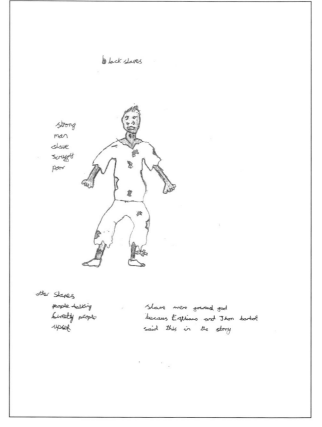

Figure 4.1 *Drawings of slaves by pupils in Year 9*

slaves dressed poorly, one is chained up, one is carrying a heavy load and two are black. From the debrief, general features about the pupils' perceptions of slaves could be drawn out as a starting point for the initial lesson. The pupils were then presented with a range of visual images showing different people from different periods of time. The pupils had to identify when they thought the pictures had been made or taken, and say whether the people in the pictures were slaves, giving reasons for their ideas. This resulted in a good degree of discussion, but helped to mould the pupils' perceptions of slaves as it was revealed that all the people pictured, from ancient and modern times, both young and old, were slaves. The activity was powerful because it started with the pupils' view of the world, got them to share their ideas, and more importantly their reasoning, before in a simple manner forcing them to reconsider their perceptions. It also acted as a very strong motivational start to the rest of the unit.

The visual images referred to here were found on the following websites:

- www.disciples.org/convo/images/Slavery.jpg

- www.historyroom.com/Slave%20Ship%20Deck.jpg

- www.msnbc.com/d/v/250x190/dl_murphy_slaves_011228.jpg

- www.camelraces.com/

- http://history1900s.about.com/library/holocaust/blpkrakow2.htm

- http://www.vroma.org/~bmcmanus/thm_man_slaves.jpg

In addition, further pictures from textbooks or other Internet sites will help give a stronger sense of slavery through time. By building up a timeline of slavery, similarities and differences can be discussed and the context of slavery can be explored, all helping to build a stronger picture of slavery before focusing on slavery in the Americas.

Such activities generate pupil talk, but a very valuable way of promoting talk in a range of circumstances is 'think, pair, share' – this is a quick way to generate ideas, as pupils are given an initial time to think and jot down some thoughts (think), they then share these with their immediate partner (pair) before finally sharing them with the class (share) – the whole process can be done in one or two minutes if needed. Too often, teachers ask questions and expect immediate responses. This can lead to the 'deathly' silence, or favours the few who are able to respond in such an environment. Giving pupils time to think and come up with ideas, which are then discussed with a partner before sharing with the class, allows for ideas to be sounded out prior to public consumption, helps pupils gain confidence, and also gives the teacher a legitimate expectation that all will have thought of a response and so anyone can be asked directly. This ensures maximum participation from a class. For example, when looking at the causes of World War I, an initial discussion prior to any input from the teacher could get pupils to come up with ideas about why fights break out, or get them to think back to previous examples of wars and why they started. This should build on the familiar and give pupils time to think.

To provide additional support, talking frames could be used. These could be displayed around the classroom, and pupils could be directed to use the most appropriate phrases. The phrases could also be grouped for ease of use.

For example, when warming up pupils' prior knowledge, they could use:

- Last lesson I remember . . .

- We learnt about . . .

- We looked at . . . this taught me . . .

When working with sources, pupils could use the following prompts:

- This tells me . . .

- In the picture I can see . . .

- This suggests . . .

- I think it was made/written/drawn in . . . because . . .

- I think it was made/written/ drawn because . . .

- Both sources say . . .

- In some ways the sources are different . . .

INSET Activity

As a department think of additional phrases that could help pupils sort their thinking through speaking frames:

1. *Think of prompts that could develop thinking about causation.*

2. *Think of prompts that develop understanding of interpretations.*

3. *Think of prompts that help pupils empathise with people in the past.*

4. *Think of prompts that get pupils thinking of change and continuity, similarity and difference.*

Teacher talk

Teacher talk also needs careful consideration, especially in terms of questioning. Questions are important in checking pupils have understood an explanation or in checking how pupils reached a particular answer: in other words, both the outcome and the process are valuable.

Checking the process by which an answer has been reached can help pupils realise how to go about working out answers in future situations, especially if this becomes an expectation of the classroom routine (Teaching Assistants can play a valuable role here – see Chapter 8, 'Managing Support').

Questions also need careful planning – both in terms of progressive difficulty and in terms of matching the objectives of the lesson. Obviously there are open and closed questions. Closed questions tend to be mainly associated with recall, factual observations, or naming someone or something. Though important in helping provide a sense of context and insight into what pupils have grasped, these types of questions are limited in what they can achieve. Often they can be the questions that are directed at the weaker pupils as they are seen as the easier sort to answer. However, for someone with a recall problem or poor attention span, they can prove particularly difficult, especially as there is generally a right or a wrong answer to the question. Failure to get the right answer can undermine a pupil's confidence (though a skilful teacher will always find a way of responding that avoids a 'put down': 'That's a good try but not quite there'; 'That's nearly right'; 'Let's see if someone else can get us a bit closer to an answer'; 'I like your thinking there, but let's try to tie that even closer to the question'; 'That's a thoughtful response, but let's take it even further now' . . .).

It is also important to use pupils' names when questioning. Not only does this ensure they are listening and prevents having to repeat a question, but for some pupils with particular needs, such as visual impairment, it is imperative the teacher clearly informs the pupil that they are about to be involved. Sometimes it can help to warn pupils quietly that they will be asked to answer a question. This gives them thinking time and allows them to answer with confidence, boosting their self-esteem.

If the aim of questioning is to warm up pupils' thinking, then it is often better to start with questions that ask pupils to recall what they did last lesson in terms of activities, e.g. 'Last lesson we were looking at slavery, what did we do?' or 'How did we find out about conditions on board slave ships?' Then pupils can be prompted to recollect what they learnt. Such an approach is far less threatening, allows pupils to use mental hooks to remember things and will elicit more successfully what pupils have retained. It also has the added benefit of getting pupils to see how different lessons link together and how knowledge or skills developed earlier can be used in a different context.

Questions that require reflection, analysis, speculation, and so on, though generally considered higher order thinking, are within the boundaries of comprehension for most pupils, with appropriate preparation. Indeed it is important to ask all pupils these questions as it provides a valuable insight into what pupils understand. The key point to bear in mind is, as Husbands 1996: 25

says: 'Pupil understanding is developed via the type of thinking which questions are intended to support.'

In history, we want to get pupils thinking about causation, consequences, change and continuity, similarity and difference, patterns in the past, inter-pretations, working with sources and so on – open questions are important in allowing pupils to address these areas. We need to think about the type of ideas we want pupils to develop and ask appropriate questions.

If we consider *causation*, we might want pupils to identify different types of causes; this could be a closed question, such as 'What economic problems led to the French Revolution?'

But to go beyond this we might ask a question that must show *greater understanding* – 'Why did the French Revolution start?'

If we want to get a more *empathetic* line of questioning we could ask 'Why did Louis XVI try to flee France?'

To elicit some form of *judgement* we need to ask 'To what extent was Louis XVI's poor government the main reason for the outbreak of revolution in France?'

The careful phrasing of questions also avoids the 'yes' or 'no' type of response and puts pupils into a position where they need to explain or justify their ideas.

Consider the following piece of text about Cromwell and the execution of Charles I, and what questions could be asked about it:

> Cromwell was a wise man. He realised that England needed a King, but a King who would rule according to the will of the people. He hoped to make Charles see reason.
>
> Then news came that Charles had again escaped and taken refuge in the Isle of Wight.
>
> Cromwell still hoped to restore the King to the throne as what is called a Constitutional Monarch, which means that laws are made by Parliament and not by the King. He had many long talks with Charles, but when he found that he was still plotting with the Scots and the French, he realised that it was hopeless.
>
> At last even Cromwell recognised the fact that whatever promises Charles made would never be kept. He agreed with the remaining members of Parliament; the King must be held guilty of all the evils which had fallen upon England as a result of his misrule . . .
>
> Cromwell tried his best to save the King's life. Charles might have remained on the throne if he had not been as stupid and obstinate as he was untrustworthy.
>
> (From the Ladybird book, *Oliver Cromwell* by L. Du Garde Peach, published in 1963.)

A host of questions could arise from this text. The simple temptation would be to use it purely for information, asking closed questions such as 'Where did Charles I escape to?' or 'Who was Charles I plotting with?' But we need to consider what type of thinking we want pupils to engage in. If causal reasoning was the main focus of the lesson, about why Charles I was executed, then we could analyse the text for this. Alternatively, we could do some interesting work on interpretations (the use of old textbooks can prove a fruitful source of interpretations work). The text offers a very distinct view of Cromwell, which could be fruitfully examined. Pupils could be asked to identify, with highlighter pen, words or phrases that show the author's opinion. Examination of further evidence could be used to judge whether the opinion has any basis in fact, or other opinions could be looked at to see how typical it is. Further work could be done, looking at why Peach may have held the view he did.

Both Husbands 1996 and Phillips 2002 have useful summaries about question types. But for pupils with special needs a bit more thought needs to be given as to how higher level reasoning can be reached – in this respect, teachers need to deliberately plan content – where particular topics are to appear, how they are to be explained, and what can be drawn on in previous work to help pupils understand the current topic.

The value of narrative

When I started teaching, my Head of Department lamented the decline of the 'good story'. It is now making something of a comeback. Stories are very useful aids to history teaching. Narrative is a common way people make sense of events – whether young or old, children with special needs or those who are deemed gifted and talented.

Stories can be used in three different ways:

1. *Telling stories* – Stories have the ability to bring the past down to a human scale, they can make the past more comprehensible and they can bring it to life. But stories only take pupils so far. The important thing to consider is what next? They can be springboards into why something happened – the death of Archduke Franz Ferdinand is a very vivid, powerful story that leads into a discussion of why his murder led to the outbreak of World War I, via a card-sorting exercise (Figure 4.2). The cards can be used to create the story leading up to the assassination, sorted into categories of relative importance etc.

2. *Writing stories* – Writing stories can be an effective way of engaging pupils and getting them to empathise with people in the past. It is a particularly tricky area, as the stories need to be based firmly in the evidence. Martin and Brooke 2002 discuss how to make effective use of fiction in the classroom. They argue that the key to successful writing is the plot. There needs to be a problem a character in the story has to resolve. Limits then need to be imposed to keep the story manageable. Restricting the number of characters can do this. In addition, there may be a time limit in which the story must take place. It is also important to be precise about the setting – this provides the historical context in which the students have to operate. Collaboration with the English department is a good way to develop the writing skills needed.

Alternatively, pupils could be asked to create a story from known facts or statements. In Figure 4.3 are a series of points drawn from contemporary accounts of the Battle of Hastings. These could be used to create an account of

1.
1908 Bosnian Crisis – Austria-Hungary took control of Bosnia, which angered both Serbia and Russia.

2.
Austria declared war on Serbia.

3.
Austria-Hungary and Russia were competing for power in the Balkans.

4.
Austria-Hungary was concerned by the growing power of Serbia.

5.
Gavrilo Princep who killed Franz Ferdinand was a Serbian terrorist.

6.
Germany declared war on Russia and prepared to attack France.

7.
Germany invaded Belgium. Britain declared war on Belgium.

8.
Germany wanted to expand and build an empire.

Figure 4.2 *Card-sorting exercise – World War I*

This is a photocopiable exercise.

9.

Germany was scared of being attacked by both France and Russia.

10.

In 1871, Germany had taken Alsace-Lorraine from France.

11.

Serbia had gained its freedom from Turkey. Serbia wanted to control all areas where Serbs lived. This included Bosnia.

12.

The Alliance System – Europe had been divided into two rival groups.

13.

The assassination of Archduke Franz Ferdinand.

14.

The Moroccan Crises of 1905 and 1911 – Germany tried to take control of Morocco from the French.

15.

The Naval Arms Race – Germany tried to build a navy to compete with Britain's.

16.

The Turkish Empire was breaking up. Lots of new countries were gaining freedom and trying to grow.

Figure 4.2 *continued*

This is a photocopiable exercise.

'Three horses were killed under him (William). Three times he leapt to his feet undaunted and swiftly avenged the death of his steed.' (William of Poitiers, c.1070)

'Yet not daring to fight on equal terms with William whom they (the Saxons) feared more than the King of Norway, they took up position on higher ground on a hill.' (William of Poitiers)

'They (the Normans) turned round and pretended to flee. Several thousand English quickly gave pursuit. The Normans suddenly turned their horses, surrounded the enemy and cut them down. Twice this trick was used with great success.' (William of Poitiers)

'Those on foot led the way . . . bearing their bows. The knights rode next, supporting the bowmen from behind.' (Robert Wace, c.1160)

'The eager courage of the Normans gave them the first strike . . . they threw spears and weapons of every kind.' (William of Poitiers)

Figure 4.3 *Creating a story from contemporary accounts*

This is a photocopiable exercise.

'The Norman foot soldiers then attacked, but it seemed they would be overwhelmed by the English missiles. Then our knights crashed into the enemy with their shields. The English remained on high ground and kept close order.' (William of Poitiers)

'The English army had a very small space; and many soldiers seeing the difficult position, deserted King Harold. Even so, he fought bravely from dawn to dusk, and the enemy's army made little impression on him until, after a great slaughter on both sides, the King fell.' (the Anglo-Saxon Chronicle)

'With the point of his lance the first knight pierced Harold's shield and chest, drenching the ground with blood. With his sword the second knight cut off his head. The third disembowelled him with his javelin. The fourth hacked off his leg.' (written by a French bishop, c.1068)

'Then it was that an arrow which was shot towards the sky, struck Harold above the right eye and that one of his eyes it put out.' (Guy of Amiens, c.1067)

Figure 4.3 *continued*

This is a photocopiable exercise.

the battle. Pupils may need to sort the events into sequence first, then decide who they want to be in the story. Further limits may be imposed by word length or how far the story can cover in time. Having written the story, pupils can compare their accounts of the battle, or even compare their accounts with a published one, like Julian Rathbone's *The Last English King* (especially pp. 372–378).

Films like Braveheart present a particular view of history

3. *Stories as sources or interpretations* – The fictionalised account of the Battle of Hastings in Julian Rathbone's *The Last English King* can lead into discussions about how accurate this version is, based on an examination of the evidence. This, in turn, can lead to discussion about why events are portrayed in certain ways. Video films can be used as stories in this respect. *Braveheart, Cromwell, Amistad* are just a few of the films that draw on history, yet each presents a particular view, for particular reasons. The Battle of Naseby as portrayed in the film *Cromwell* bears no relation to the actual events that happened. Having given pupils an account of the battle, they can then have fun trying to spot the errors in the film. They can then be led into an exploration of why the film offers a certain view.

Inclusive approaches to teaching

Besides being very conscious of how he uses language, the history teacher needs to consider other key factors in the creation of an inclusive classroom: engagement; building up of contextual knowledge; and the construction of tasks.

Engaging pupils

Those who have attended in-service training from Michael Riley about 'hooking' pupils into activities or read the late Rob Phillips' article about 'Initial Stimulus Material' will need no telling about the power of captivating and motivating pupils. Given a strong enough stimulus, pupils will tackle the most difficult of topics with enthusiasm.

One such 'hook' created by Michael Riley is based on the story of the death of Abbot Richard Whiting in 1539. It is a gripping tale, which even notoriously poor storytellers like me can make compelling. Dimming the lights, and telling the pupils that they are about to hear a dreadful tale of death helps set the scene and gets the pupils listening expectantly. Use of small details helps to conjure up recognisable images in the pupils' minds that finally culminate in the graphic details of Whiting's last few moments. Having got them engrossed, the class will readily engage in a card-sort activity to explain the reasons behind his death. The result is the start of an understanding of the background to the Dissolution of the Monasteries and the entire motives behind the English Reformation.

Do the pupils need differentiated materials to tackle this? In most cases they do not: the process of engagement has got the class wanting to find out more, and that is a far more powerful means of getting pupils to learn than simply giving them different resources or worksheets to complete.

There are other means of engaging pupils: the 'sex, death and toilet' approach to history has its merits in this area, but so do mysteries, storytelling, and visual puzzles. Trying to get pupils to work out what is happening in Cruickshank's depiction of the Peterloo Massacre *Manchester Heroes* is a powerful way into C19th politics (see Figure 4.4). The picture is suitable for a layers of inference

Figure 4.4 Manchester Heroes *by Cruickshank*

approach. Pupils need to say what they can see, and try to suggest what they think is happening. Then they can ask questions for the teacher to answer. They become intrigued by the passions that were aroused by something they see as mundane. An introduction to medieval perceptions of heaven and hell can be done by looking at one small detail in a medieval doom painting, and discussing what they think the picture depicts and what else they think might be in the rest of the picture. Then the class can piece together the bigger picture which has been cut up and made into a jigsaw puzzle – this allows for pupils to test their initial ideas and use clues within the picture to piece it together before contrasting their initial perceptions of the whole picture with their own. This, in turn, can lead into a general discussion about what the picture shows and what insights it gives into the medieval mind. Most textbooks on medieval Britain contain such images that could be copied, or there are websites that contain suitable material such as: http://www.godecookery.com/macabre/gallery4/macbr120.jpg

A graphic way to gain the attention of a class studying the prohibition is to pour a bottle of wine into a bucket at the start of a lesson! Such starter activities are a crucial element in getting pupils 'on side' at the start of a lesson and wanting to engage and participate.

INSET Activity

As a department, draw up a list of different possible starter activities. Start with one unit and create a series of starters. Then see which of them could be used for a different topic and, in this way, gradually build up a bank of ideas. Consider how these starters might engage the attention of pupils with a range of different difficulties.

Teaching and learning styles

Much has been made of Gardner's theory of multiple intelligences, and the idea that pupils learn in different ways. Teachers teach in different ways, and it is important for you to recognise how you teach and what style you actually use in order to see how well you are meeting the different learning needs of the pupils in your history class.

The most useful and common learning styles to consider are visual, auditory and kinaesthetic. Traditional teaching styles tend to favour auditory learners, and it may well be that teachers who are the successful product of such a system tend to have a natural bias towards auditory teaching styles. What then do we need to do to meet the range of learning styles within a classroom?

Case study – Steven, a pupil with ADHD

'Steve' has been diagnosed with ADHD. Though prescribed Ritalin, this has been stopped as the drug was stunting his growth. He finds concentrating on a task for any length of time difficult. He interrupts the lesson by calling out and by asking unnecessary questions. He aggravates other pupils by saying unkind things and consequently is unpopular with his peers. He is very impulsive and lacks concentration. He has little social awareness and blames others for his inability to make friends. He finds it difficult to resist reacting to comments from other pupils and there have been incidents where he has hit others with little provocation. He is very disorganised and tends to carry a lot of equipment with him, which makes it difficult for him to find what he wants at the start of a lesson.

Strengths
Steve enjoys physical activities, as well as drama, singing and dancing. He is able verbally and likes working on computers.

General IEP targets:
- to settle down quickly at the start of the lesson – teacher could have box of equipment ready specially for Steve with all he needs in it;
- to improve social skills and to work co-operatively with others – has TA support – teacher to encourage pair work;
- to complete all work on time.

Lesson background:
The class had started work on WWI. At this stage, they had looked at the causes of the war, including the story of the assassination of Archduke Franz Ferdinand, which caught Steve's interest. The class had subsequently looked at the failure of the Schlieffen Plan, and was at this point ready to move on to trench warfare.

Lesson objectives:
The pupils will be able to:
- identify different types of weapons used in WWI;
- explain why the defensive side had the advantage for most of the war;
- explain which weapons they feel had the most/least impact on the fighting in the war.

Steve's objectives for this lesson:
- to wait until asked to answer a question or to ask a question;
- to work co-operatively with another pupil to produce a PowerPoint presentation explaining which weapons had the most/least impact on the fighting.

Activities:

Prior to the lesson, someone talked through the lesson plan with Steve so he knew what to expect. Another possibility would have been to provide Steve with an outline of what would be covered with timings shown.

1. At the start of the lesson, the teacher showed a brief clip from the original film version of *All Quiet on the Western Front*. This showed a short but dramatic scene from an attack by French troops on the German lines. The class then had to identify different weapons they had seen in the film and what questions they would like to ask about the weapons they had seen. The TA worked with Steve, and recorded his answers for him. Steve produced a list of questions with the TA.

2. The teacher asked for feedback. On the board she wrote a list of weapons seen, then recorded questions the pupils had. The TA helped Steve wait his turn until he was asked.

3. The pupils were then given an information sheet about weapons in WWI, and working in pairs had to see how many of their own questions they could answer. Steve again worked with the TA. The teacher praised Steve for his patience to date while circulating round the class. She also checked his answers and where he had produced a good idea, she indicated she wanted him to say this when she asked a particular question.

4. The teacher asked for feedback. Steve again had to wait his turn, with the TA there to help keep him focused.

5. The pupils were asked to focus on the information sheet again, looking at the section about advantages and disadvantages of different types of weapons. To help Steve, he was given a sheet where he could do a heads and tails exercise to match pros and cons with particular weapons. The TA worked alongside Steve during this.

6. Pupils were then paired up. They had to decide between themselves which weapons they thought were most effective and least effective, and whether the weapons favoured the attacking or defending side in WWI. They had to produce a presentation explaining their ideas. There were three laptops available in the classroom, so Steve and his partner were given one to produce a PowerPoint presentation. The TA worked with Steve and his partner. The work was to be finished for homework. Steve agreed to do the weapons that were most effective, and his partner did those that were least effective. The TA was to help Steve complete his work in homework club that evening.

Points to note about the lesson

The lesson had a number of activities, which added pace and avoided the problem of an activity going on too long. The video sequence at the start attracted Steve's attention, and the idea of the pupils creating questions allowed them to feel a greater sense of ownership of the lesson. In addition, the support from the TA and the teacher's praise part way through the lesson helped encourage concentration. The use of ICT for Steve played to another of his interests, and the fact that he was to use one of the laptops made working with him more attractive.

Visual learners

Visual learners learn by seeing or by having large chunks of text or spoken work broken down into smaller, more manageable sections. Diagrams, cartoons, pictures, tables, presentations and so on are more likely to succeed with such pupils. I don't remember much from my school days in the history lesson, but I do remember the cartoons in the *History Alive* series by Peter Moss, and all my colleagues from a similar era likewise remember them. Why? Because they provided simple images to retain, yet contained a number of key ideas.

Ideas for use with visual learners:

- *Pictures* – Get visual learners to summarise ideas into some sort of a picture rather than into written notes, e.g. when looking at important individuals, get them to produce a series of portraits for a 'Hall of Fame' where the person's achievements need to be included within the picture.

- *Modified visual sources* – Get pupils to demonstrate how something has changed: use an image of the situation prior to an event, then get the pupils to redraw it after the event, e.g. show a scene in a nineteenth-century factory prior to the reform acts, then redraw the scene following the reform acts.

- *Comparison of visual sources* – Compare visual sources from different times to create a sense of similarity and difference, change and continuity.

- *Graphs* – Convert information into graphs, and get the pupils to then explain what patterns the data shows.

- *Timelines* – Construct timelines that use visual images to show developments across a period. This can be extended by the use of parallel timelines, for example; timelines showing developments in transport 1750–1900, can be put alongside a timeline of agricultural changes, and developments in the iron industry, coal industry and so on (see Figure 4.5). Pupils can then be challenged to make links between the timelines.

- *Tables* – Large chunks of text can be easily broken down and put into sections of a table, e.g. pupils might identify different reasons for the Roman invasion of Britain and put them under the appropriate heading in a table (see Figure 4.6).

- *Diagrams* – Ripple diagrams can be used to show the impact of an event or situation, e.g. the impact of hyperinflation in Weimar Germany can be examined by looking at a number of case studies, with those most badly affected being placed at the centre of the diagram, and those less badly affected being placed towards the outside. Flow diagrams are another way to make chunks of text more manageable, as pupils can break the story down into the essential steps. Causes and consequences of events such as the Agricultural Revolution can be summarised succinctly (see Figure 4.7).

- *Storyboards* – Pupils could convert a piece of text into a storyboard sequence or explain what they think has happened prior to the event in a picture, and what they think happens after the picture.

DATE	FARMING	TEXTILES	COAL	IRON	TRANSPORT
1700			1700 – 2.75 million tonnes of coal dug	c.1700 Crisis shortage of charcoal supplies	
1710			1708 – Newcomen's steam pump	1709 Abraham Darby I used coke to smelt iron ore	
1730	c.1730 – work of 'Turnip' Townshend; 1731 – Jethro Tull published 'Horse-hoeing Husbandry'	1733 – Kay's Flying Shuttle		1738–1763 – work of Abraham Darby II	
1750	Improvements in livestock				1750s/1760s – turnpike boom; 1761 – Bridgewater Canal
1760		1764 – Hargreaves' Spinning Jenny; 1769 – Arkwright's water frame		1766 Cranage's invent reverbatory furnace	
1770	1770s/1780s – Arthur Young publicised new farming ideas	1779 – Crompton's Mule; 1785 – Cartwright's Power Loom		1779 – ironbridge built by Abraham Darby III; 1784 – Cort's puddling and rolling process	
1780					
1790	1793 – war with France led to less food imports				1790s – canal mania; 1790s/1800s – golden age of coaching
1800			1800 – 10 million tonnes of coal dug; 1807 Buddle's air pump		
1810					
1830	By 1820 most land in East Anglia and Midlands had been enclosed		1815 – Davy's safety lamp		1825 – Stockton and Darlington railway; 1830 – opening of Liverpool and Manchester railway
1850			1850 – 50 million tonnes of coal dug		

Figure 4.5 *Parallel timelines*

Emperor Claudius had been treated as an idiot most of his life. He wanted to be seen as a successful emperor.

Certain groups, such as Druids, had been stirring up trouble in Gaul.

Britain produced valuable wheat, metals and other goods.

A military victory would be a good way to win the loyalty of the Roman people.

By conquering Britain, it would be easier to protect the northern edge of the Empire from attack.

A British tribe, the Atrebates, sent a delegation to see Claudius to ask for help against the Catuvellauni.

The British tribes were divided and would be easy to beat.

(NB Some points could go under more than one heading – this creates an opportunity for pupils to discuss the appropriateness of the headings, and possibly suggest alternative ways of organising the different reasons.)

Figure 4.6 *Card-sorting exercise – the Roman invasion of Britain*

This is a photocopiable exercise.

Things to do with Claudius	Things to do with Britain	Things to do with strengthening the Empire

Figure 4.6 *continued*

Use the statement cards on p. 63 sorted into causes and consequences – perhaps on post-it notes – to make a poster.

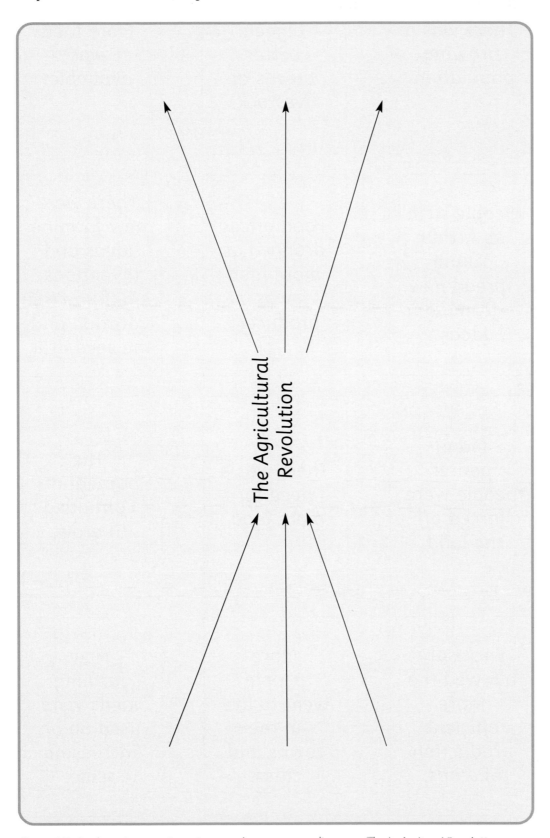

Figure 4.7 *Card-sorting exercise – Cause and consequence diagram – The Agricultural Revolution*

This is a photocopiable exercise.

There was a growing population.	There were bigger, better breeds of livestock.	More food was available.
People such as Arthur Young spread new farming ideas.	Food prices dropped as more food was produced.	There were new farming ideas and inventions, e.g. four-crop rotation and the seed drill.
Many poorer people were forced off the land.	There was a need for more food.	The population continued to grow.
Enclosure allowed the more efficient production of crops.	More people went to live in the towns and cities.	New farming ideas were used on an increasing scale.

Figure 4.7 *continued*

This is a photocopiable exercise.

Case study – Kuli, a pupil with HI

Kuli is in Year 7. He has significant hearing loss. He has some hearing in his right ear but is heavily reliant on his hearing aid and visual clues ranging from lip reading to body language and facial expression to get the gist and tone of what people are saying. This means he can find lessons tiring and often misses crucial details. Reading is a useful alternative input and his mechanical reading skills are good but he does not always get the full message because of language delay. He has problems with new vocabulary and with asking and responding to questions. He follows most lessons as the rest of his tutor group, but he does receive some individual support from a teacher of the deaf.

Kuli has a good sense of humour but appreciates visual jokes more readily. He is very literal and is puzzled by all sorts of idiom. He was shocked when he heard that someone had been 'painting the town red' as he thought this was some act of vandalism! Even though he often knows what he wants to say he finds it difficult to express his ideas readily.

Although Kuli is a very pleasant and friendly individual, he is not really part of any group as he finds it hard to follow what is said and can misunderstand what other children say. He has a Teaching Assistant, which also marks him out as different. There is a danger that he may become increasingly frustrated by his difficulties and 'switch off'.

Strengths:
Kuli is very organised. When he has been able to access a topic he is able to demonstrate a good level of understanding. He likes drawing and physical activity, where he can do something on his own, such as running.

General IEP targets:
- to ensure instructions are understood – repeat to another person in the class what needs to be done;
- to develop oral confidence – to answer at least one question per lesson;
- to work with another pupil in paired work to improve social confidence.

Lesson background:
The lesson is about the problems between the Monarchy and Church in medieval England. It will focus on the case of Henry II and Thomas Becket. Prior to this lesson, pupils had studied the role of kings and the extent of their power, particularly in relation to the nobility. In addition, the class had done some work on the role of the Church in medieval life. For homework, the pupils had been given a photocopied section from the textbook that looked at the arguments between Henry II and Becket, prior to Becket's murder (at this stage, the pupils did not know what the outcome of the story would be).

Lesson objectives:
The pupils will be able to:
- give several reasons why Becket was murdered, and in some cases use their prior knowledge to explain the reason for the crisis; discuss different ways they could categorise these reasons, and decide which would be most appropriate for organising a piece of extended writing;
- in some cases, be able to explain who was the winner from the murder of Becket – Becket or Henry II, Monarchy or Church?

Kuli's objectives for this lesson:
- to repeat instructions to his TA to ensure he has understood the work;
- to work alongside another pupil and discuss reasons why Becket was murdered and to categorise these reasons;

- to record his ideas in a manner that demonstrates his understanding, either as a table, diagram or mind-map.

Activities:

(Prior to the lesson, Kuli had used one of his individual support sessions to go through the story of Becket and Henry II, which he had turned into a storyboard.)

1. The teacher ensured understanding of the homework by asking the class to speculate about what they thought would happen next in the story, and why. The pupils had to write down no more than five words to explain what they thought would happen or draw a quick picture. The TA ensured Kuli had understood the task, and observed as he drew a quick sketch of a fight between Henry and Becket.

2. The teacher then read Edward Grim's account of the murder of Becket in a dramatic fashion. While reading out the account, selected pupils acted out what happened. Kuli watched what happened.

3. The pupils were then challenged to explain why Becket was murdered. The pupils, working in pairs, were prompted to go back to their reading homework and search for possible reasons. The pupils recorded their ideas as bullet points or mind-maps. The TA worked alongside Kuli and another pupil as they went through their homework, picking out reasons. (Kuli's storyboard helped both pupils identify a number of reasons.)

4. These reasons were then discussed as a class. Kuli offered a reason, encouraged by the TA. The teacher then used questioning to get pupils to make links with their prior learning. These ideas were recorded on the board. The TA worked with Kuli, helping him find information in his exercise book that was appropriate.

5. Pupils were then reminded of earlier work they had done on categorising causes when they had studied the reasons for the success of the Roman army. In pairs again, pupils were asked to categorise these different reasons. The TA observed Kuli as he worked alongside his earlier partner. They decided to use a mind-map and colour coded those reasons that were linked in some way. Once the TA was happy Kuli was able to work with his partner, she went to work with other pupils in the class. Those that finished early were encouraged to speculate about who gained from this incident. (This would be the main focus of the next lesson.)

6. These different categories were discussed, and pupils were questioned about which would be the most appropriate way to organise them for writing an answer to the question 'Why was Becket brutally murdered?' Homework was set that got pupils to plan a draft answer to this question by writing topic sentences, followed by one or two examples to include in each paragraph.

Points to note about the lesson

The lesson helped Kuli in a number of ways. Firstly he was able to access the material. The homework and preparation time meant he was able to participate and understand the opening part of the lesson. With Grim's account of Becket's murder and pupils acting it out, Kuli was able to understand clearly what had happened, as the visual action reinforced what the teacher read. The early discussion and thinking work was geared towards Kuli's needs, as he had support from the TA who could check his understanding. He was able to record his work in a manner most accessible to him, and he gained confidence as his preparation prior to the lesson meant he was in a position to help his partner. Later in the lesson, once the TA was happy he was coping, she was able to leave him to work with others, which helped his self-esteem, as he was not the only person who was seen to be 'needing' support.

Auditory learners

The principal characteristic of the auditory learner is that aural stimulus provides the quickest and most direct way to the limbic system and thereby to the retentive memory. The effect of this is that classroom activities based on listening and speaking are those most likely to allow such pupils to access the skill, concept or fact being taught. Since many special needs pupils have been identified as such by their difficulty in reading text, auditory techniques are doubly valuable:

- as the primary method of learning for the genuine auditory learner;

- as an additional method of access for the child whose special need is that of overcoming great difficulty in accessing written text.

Since history classrooms have traditionally relied heavily on written sources of evidence, any history teacher seeking to use auditory techniques may have to convert visual or textual material into aural stimulus.

Other resources such as music or spoken word interviews do, of course, lend themselves directly to the auditory learner, and the pupil will have direct access to the inflexion and intonation of voice (and thereby to the intentions and possible unconscious prejudice of the speaker), or to the raw emotional power of music. Well-selected auditory materials can have immense impact on all pupils, as well as particular powers of inclusion for those whose preferred or natural learning style is auditory.

Never underestimate the power of an auditory source. Few people can remain detached from one of Churchill's wartime speeches or from the sobs of an evacuee on a newsreel. A radio play involves the listener and requires that he or she actively construct characters and scenes mentally – thereby joining the author in an active role rather than passively accepting the interpretations of others from a video source. Likewise, a powerful song of historical experience can access the emotions as well or better than any straight text: songs, for example, such as Elton John's *Indian Sunset*, describing the experiences of an Indian warrior in the American West of the 1870s. How effectively the despair of the Great Depression can be brought alive either by Billy Bragg's *Between the Wars* or Bing Crosby's rendition of *Buddy Can You Spare a Dime!* In many ways, bearing in mind the needs of the auditory learner can benefit the whole class. The potential is immense. Here are a few introductory ideas to begin to realise that potential.

Ideas for use with auditory learners:

- Find a song or piece of music connected to the historical topic being taught. This can be used as a piece of Initial Stimulus Material (Phillips, 2001) to engage pupils from a very early stage in studying a topic. Music can also create emotions in a listener and provide access to the intentions or feelings of the composer. Emotional engagement is the key to placing a youngster 'inside' a topic rather than undertaking detached study from the outside – the difference between window shopping and actual purchase. Lyrics can provide factual information, material for interpretation – or both as in *The Green Fields of France* written by E. Bogle and performed by the Furey brothers. Here, the events of the Battle of the Somme are both described and interpreted in an unequivocal way. As the sound of such a song dies away, pupils can be invited to describe their immediate reaction aloud in one word or a short phrase. Do all of them react in the same way? How do we explain any differences? Here we have an exercise for discussion and a case study in interpretation all in one. What of their views as to the intention of the composer? What in the song led to such a view and can a pupil give a justification – however simple? Much historical music is available from the Past Times stores now found in virtually every high street. Suggestions are given in Figure 4.8. Many of the pieces below will be available to order by any good CD shop.

- Use your own voice to read a source aloud several times using alternative emphasis, tone or vocal interpretation of the piece. Ask pupils to express an opinion as to which reading was closest to the original intention of the piece and insist upon a justification! A Churcillian quotation read out in a jovial manner will not ring true – asking pupils why not asks them to match content with tone in an oral cross-referencing exercise.

- Play a video clip with the sound turned down then with alternative musical accompaniment from a CD player. Which piece of music expresses the mood or intention of the film best and why? For example, play a piece of rousing marshal music to a clip from *All Quiet on the Western Front*, and then play a ballad such as *Green Fields of France*. A group could also discuss the way each piece of accompaniment changes the overall effect of the source, e.g. Helen Reddy's *Woman* could accompany Emily Davison's death at the Derby on film, then pupils could listen to John Lennon's very different song of the same name.

- Don't neglect the radio schedules for historically useful programmes. There are many documentaries, interviews and readings of historical works or novels that can be immensely valuable in the classroom. The mental pictures required of the auditory learner can be an invaluable bridge between auditory and visual learning styles. The readings of source material in the Radio 4 series *This Sceptred Isle* were unforgettable. Tape recordings can be collected as part of the department's resource bank. No time to organise and oversee recording? Enlist the help of someone's parent or grandparent – send out a request with pupils or ask at parents' evenings.

Study Unit	Suggested Music
Britain 1066–1500	*Gregorian Chant*, Medieval Music. (Medieval Church and Court); *Flower of Scotland* (Edward II)
Britain 1500–1750	Tudor music (Court of Henry VIII); *Flowers of the Forest* (Battle of Flodden); *The World Turned Upside-Down* (Diggers); *Lily Bolero* (The Boyne); Handel's *Music for the Royal Fireworks* (Hanoverians)
Britain 1750–1900	Sea shanties (trade and commerce); *Rule Britannia* or Noel Coward's *Mad Dogs and Englishmen* (British Empire); *Artificial Flowers* by the Beautiful South (Victorian social conditions)
A European Study Before 1914	*Le Marseillaise*, *1812 Overture* or Beethoven's *Symphony No. 3* ('Eroica') (French Revolution)
A World Study Before 1914	*John Brown's Body*, *Dixie*, or any black spiritual music (Black Peoples of the Americas) *Indian Sunset* by Elton John (Plains Indians)
A World Study After 1914	Any song of the Great War, *We'll Meet Again* or *Bluebirds Over* by Vera Lynn. *Lili Marlene* by Marlene Dietrich (World War II); *Thoroughly Modern Millie* by Julie Andrews (Emancipation of Women); *Between the Wars* by Billy Bragg or *Buddy Can You Spare a Dime?* (Depression); Any 1960s protest song such as *Times They are a Changing* by Bob Dylan or *Universal Soldier* by Donovan (Post WW2)

Figure 4.8 *Music connected with historical topics*

- Use distinctive sounds – after a study of context – to deduce likely reactions from contemporaries. What differing reactions, for example, would we get from a survivor of World War II by playing the 'Take Cover' siren then the 'All Clear'? What different reactions would 'Stop thief!' bring about in a Victorian gentleman or a street urchin of the same period? How about, 'Bring out your dead' to a medieval traveller, or 'Land Ho!' to a sailor with Cook? What does a church bell mean now? In 1940? In 738 on Lindisfarne?

- Invite an older person who lived through the events of the twentieth century into school to talk about his or her experiences. (Hold a previous interview with the old person to give a clear brief as to what you want covered. This will avoid aimless rambling guaranteed to turn off even the most avid auditory learners!). Invite groups to compose questions of their own for the visitors to be delivered aloud. (It is wise to stage a dry run in case of inappropriate questions.) Be sure also to schedule a downstairs room close to the school entrance for such an activity. Elderly visitors rarely take kindly to a corridor full of adolescents or to long flights of stairs. I, early in my career, nearly caused the early demise of several survivors of the Normandy landings by booking an upstairs room 150 metres from the entrance to the building.

- Read a poem aloud to the class. Poems of contrasting moods can lead to fascinating discussion. Compare, for example, Rupert Brooke's *The Soldier* with his sonnet *Peace*. Even mood within the same poem can change as in John Mac Rae's *In Flanders Fields*. Pair pupils – each to read the same line of a poem to each other. How were the readings different or similar?

- Stage a competitive debate. Two teams will explore both sides of a controversial issue, then will be told to argue for one position only. For example, one side might argue that life in a cotton factory was fair and reasonable, whereas the other would argue that this was not the case. Marks can be scored for well-made historical points in support of a position, or for successful challenges to one of the other side's arguments. For full details of such a debate please see my article in *Teaching History* 105 (Luff, 2001).

- Assign the class a role as a committee discussing a particular issue – health and safety in a nineteenth-century factory, for example, or a railway board deciding if horses or locomotives should pull their trains.

- Compose a 'living graph' from a reading of a historically related text or source. Pupils could mark rise and fall of emotion over time, for example on a simple graph axis, as the teacher reads an account of life as an evacuee or as a job seeker in Jarrow.

- Read a provocative statement about an historical figure the class has studied and ask a pupil for a quick 'gut reaction' response and brief justification for that response. Teacher: 'Custer was an arrogant fool'; Pupil: 'No, he wasn't. How could he have known how many Indians there were?' However primitive the response, the need for justification will underline one of the main skills of historical study.

- Introduce the talking essay. Split the class into groups, each with a spokesperson. The group should come up with a relevant 'because' or causation statement in answer to a 'why' question from a given category, such as long-term factors, trigger factors or chance. Spokespersons should read aloud their statement. The class should vote on the most effective order of statements for maximum impact.

- Role play and practical demonstration can make a huge impact on all types of learner. Please see Chapter 6 which deals with this teaching technique.

Case study – Josie, a pupil with VI

Josie has very little useful sight. She uses a stick to get around school and some of the other children make cruel comments about this, which she finds hurtful. She also wears glasses with very thick lenses, which she hates. On a number of occasions she has been knocked over in the corridor but insists these were accidents rather than incidents of bullying. She may, however, be unable to recognise pupils who do pick on her.

Now in Year 9, Josie is growing ever conscious that she is different. She has specialist equipment such as talking scales in food technology and a CCTV for use with textbooks, but dislikes using it at times. Her classmates tolerate her but there is little social interaction, as she cannot make eye contact with others.

She has a reading age approximately three years behind her chronological age and spells phonetically. Many of the teaching strategies used to make learning more interesting disadvantage her. The layout of certain books in history with colourful double page spreads, and text interspersed with cartoons and sources, makes it very difficult for her to follow, even with her CCTV or an enlarged photocopy of the text, as she cannot track which bit goes where. She got very bored one day, when every lesson she had, made extensive use of videos, which she was unable to benefit from.

Strengths:

Josie is able to utilise her other senses well. In art she has enjoyed the lessons where she has been given opportunities to work in 3-D; she enjoys listening to music and has a well-developed sense of rhythm. She enjoys physical activity outside of school, but feels insecure in school where there are large numbers of people moving around and classrooms tend to be cramped for space.

General IEP targets:

- to boost self-confidence by allowing participation in lessons through suitable activities;
- to work co-operatively with other pupils;
- to contribute orally in lessons at least once.

Lesson background:

Year 9 have been doing work on the First World War. They have covered the causes of the war, the creation of stalemate on the Western Front, and are now starting to explore life in the trenches. The teacher is keen to use this topic as an opportunity to develop pupils' source skills. This will take place over two lessons.

Lesson objectives:

The pupils will be able to:

- make inferences from the sources;
- make decisions about the usefulness of sources for a line of enquiry;

- decide which objects to include in a class museum about WWI and justify their choice.

Josie's objectives for this lesson:
- to work co-operatively with other pupils;
- to demonstrate her understanding of inference and tone orally;
- to select three objects for the class museum and explain her criteria for choice.

Activities:

1. The pupils, in twos and threes, were asked to brainstorm all they knew about WWI. Josie worked with another pupil and with a TA. All ideas were recorded on sugar paper.

2. These ideas were fed back to the teacher who recorded them on the board. The teacher then asked the pupils, 'How do we know about the First World War?' Pupils were given a couple of minutes to discuss ideas before feeding back to the teacher. Josie discussed her ideas with the other pupils, which was again recorded by the TA on the back of the sugar paper. Josie was encouraged to contribute by the TA.

3. The teacher then asked the class which of these pieces of evidence would be most useful in finding out about the life of an ordinary soldier in the First World War. At this stage the teacher wanted an initial 'gut' reaction.

4. The teacher explained that the class would then examine a range of sources, using layers of inference diagrams (which they had used previously in Year 8). The teacher modelled an example of a poem. She read it out once, and then gave pupils their own copies to read (Josie had a large photocopy). The teacher then read it again. Pupils then started to discuss ideas in their small groups about what this source told them, what it suggested, and what it didn't tell them. They fed ideas back to the teacher who recorded key points on the board. The teacher then gave pupils a word bank to help them understand the tone of the source. Once the teacher was sure the pupils were secure in their understanding of the work, she distributed a range of sources to different groups of pupils.

5. Josie and her partner were given two things. One was a WWI replica helmet. Josie was able to touch the object and use this sense to analyse the source. Josie and her partner discussed their ideas, which the TA recorded. The other item was a recording of a WWI soldiers' song. Josie and her partner were able to listen to this on a tape recorder with headphones. They were able to discuss their ideas and the TA again recorded them.

6. Near the end of the lesson, one person from each group had to go to a different group to find out what they had been analysing. Josie stayed in her place, and then had to explain to another pupil what she had discovered from her sources.

7. At the end, pupils fed back briefly about what they had learnt from the sources, and reconsidered their earlier 'gut' reaction about which sources would be most useful (the teacher planned to use this as the starting point for the next lesson as well).

In the following lesson, the pupils would get further opportunities to discuss their work and compare different pieces of evidence. In small groups, the pupils would have to decide what objects to include in their display, and why.

Points to note about the lesson:

Josie benefited from this lesson in a number of ways. The amount of text-based work was limited, and where it was used, in the case of the poem, it could be blown up easily and was uncluttered. The use of the TA to support recording of information removed this obstacle during this lesson and allowed Josie to concentrate on the key objectives of the lesson, namely consideration of sources. The type of sources she used allowed her to access them using different senses, and near the end she took on the role of 'expert' when she told another pupil about her two sources. This helped her sense of self-esteem, and allowed others to see her in a positive light.

Kinaesthetic learners

Do you have pupils who constantly fidget and cannot keep still or be quiet? The likelihood is that they are kinaesthetic learners. Such pupils need to move. The idea of sitting behind a table for an hour, in an uncomfortable chair, being told to be quiet and listen carefully is not the ideal way for these pupils to learn. Change in pace of the lesson and activities are important, as are activities that allow them the chance to try things out physically.

Ideas for use with Kinaesthetic learners:

● *Human continuums* – Get pupils to place themselves across an imaginary line in the classroom to show understanding of an issue or their opinion. For example, pupils might be assigned as a political party in the Weimar Republic, with a description of the beliefs of that party. They then have to decide where their party stands on a political spectrum from the extreme right to extreme left. This can allow pupils to develop a greater sense of political knowledge and of the characteristics of different political parties as they are questioned about why they have chosen their position, who they might work alongside and why. Alternatively, pupils might be asked to show an opinion about whom they feel was the worst medieval monarch. Having been given individual monarchs, they might stand on a worst to best continuum, and have to justify why they have placed their monarch in such a position.

● *Social order* – One of the key ideas that pupils need to pick up about the past is the differing social structures that existed. By giving out role cards with different characters on, pupils have to negotiate themselves into a line of social order.

- *Human or 'talking' essays* – Instead of writing essays, get pupils to talk their way through one. To help them get used to the idea of 'big' and 'little' points, distribute a series of sentences around the class to each child. They then have to find the rest of their paragraph and put themselves together into a coherent order. Then they have to communicate their paragraph to the rest of the class. The class can then sort the groups out into a suitable order to create a coherent overall essay.

- *Acting out a source* – Reading can be a problem for many children. This is a major difficulty, especially if we want them to pick out the significance of certain points or wish the class to remember the passage. Acting out the text can provide a better prompt for the memory than just listening. Have props ready, as well as questions to highlight key ideas. For the history of medicine, a pestle and mortar, a sheet, and some honey and dates can be used very simply in helping retell the story of what happened in an Ancient Greek Asclepion, when the god, Asclepios, supposedly visited the patients in the night to cure them.

- *Reading/Acting out the tone of a source* – Pupils have to identify the key words in a text that give the tone of the source, hence its meaning as well. Pupils can then be asked to read or act the source out in that tone. For example, the following extract from a letter by an officer involved in the Battle of the Somme, describes the actions of Captain Wilfred Neville to his sister:

  > Five minutes before zero time, your brother strolled up in his usual calm way and we shared a joke before going over. The company went over very well, with Soames and your brother kicking off with company footballs. We had to face very heavy rifle and machine gun fire and nearing the front German trench, the line slackened pace slightly. Seeing this Wilfred dashed forward with a bomb in his hand . . .

  Key words like 'calm' and 'dashed' give particular impressions of the way Neville acted. By picking these out, pupils could then act out his actions before he tragically died, in the manner of these words. Alternatives could be introduced, such as 'agitated' and 'crept', which could be acted out or read in a particular tone. This would show how particular words can dramatically transform the meaning of something that is written.

- *Card sorting* – This is a simple means of allowing pupils to manipulate text physically, thereby allowing them to play with ideas without penalty, because if the ideas don't fit or need modification, then something can be done about it.

- *'Pendulum of change'* – To get across the idea of change within a period, pupils could move around the class to demonstrate this. When looking, for example, at the religious changes of the sixteenth century, a continuum from Roman Catholic to Puritan could be set up, and pupils could move to different areas of the class, depending on who was ruling. A trainee of mine found the school playground was the ideal place to carry out such an activity! To bring an extra edge to this, certain artefacts could be placed in the centre of the classroom, and every time there was a change of ruler, pupils would have to pick up or jettison items depending on whether they would be allowed under the new monarch.

- *'Who's my friend?'* – This activity can be carried out where pupils have to create different sides in a conflict. When examining the outbreak of WWI, cards describing different problems between the Great Powers can be handed out, and the pupils assigned to individual countries. They then have to work out who they can side with, and form two sides. From this they can be quizzed about the choice of their allies and why they oppose the other countries.

INSET Activity

As a department, take a scheme of work, and examine individual lesson plans. Highlight where visual, auditory and kinaesthetic approaches occur in a) lessons b) the scheme of work as a whole. Where one of these is missing or given less emphasis, see where you could build in one of the suggested ideas above or other ideas of your own to cater for the full range of learning styles consistently.

Accessible, but challenging

Accessibility is fundamental to success in learning. Peter Fisher, in his article on teaching about Anne Frank, talks of starting with the familiar, before leading pupils into new learning, or what Vygotsky terms the pupil's 'zone of proximal development'. Start the pupils with somewhere that is known and comfortable before extending them and taking them on their learning journey. When studying witchcraft, ask the class to draw a picture of a witch as a starter. You can imagine readily the black pointy hats, the black cat, the broomstick, and so on. It provides a nice safe starting point but can lead into interesting discussion about where such stereotypical images come from before going on to compare the reality of who witches were and what they were like.

Visual images also provide a readily accessible format for pupils as long as they are guided into the meaning of the image via careful questioning. Using the ideas of getting pupils to state what they can see, then going on to what the picture suggests is very simple but effective. The following example shows how a trainee teacher skilfully moved a low set of Year 8 pupils from their own perceptions about rights, through a visual image, into people's status and rights in the French Revolution, then into some detailed work about the Declaration of the Rights of Man, before coming back to the initial visual image:

1   The lesson started with the familiar: what rights do you as Year 8 have today? This generated a number of points from the right to a break time to 'the right to say what you want without persecution' (the pupil's words not mine!).

2 Then it moved onto a discussion of a cartoon, showing members of the first two estates standing on a rock, on top of someone from the third estate. The pupils then had to describe what they could see in the picture before explaining its message by drawing on their prior knowledge. This stage was important in helping the pupils make sense of the next step.

3 In pairs, the pupils were then asked to read one of the terms from the 'Declaration of the Rights of Man' and summarise it in three to five words to record on the board. This was achieved by all pupils, who could then relate their prior knowledge of the problems in France to the Declaration, to see why each term existed. This showed that they had made the links between what had gone on in the period prior to the Revolution and the circumstances of the Declaration.

4 To round off the lesson, pupils had to redraw the cartoon but from a perspective after the Declaration, to show how the social order would look differently. The beauty of the lesson was in its simplicity. Every task was accessible but led to pupils making real strides forward in their understanding of the period.

The following example shows how a mixed-ability class can have access to material that at the same time offers serious challenge to all (it has been adapted from a task contained in *Practical History* Series 1 1995/6 January issue, published by Stanley Thornes). The common task is deceptively simple. The pupils have to produce a written account of Charles I's execution. It is essentially a descriptive piece of writing, but it must be based on the evidence, much of which is contradictory. This is where the open-ended, but structured, challenge comes in. Crucially, the task is accessible to all. The pupils have to complete a grid (see Figure 4.9), drawing information from the sources (see pages 80–1).

The table is simple to complete. The sources are accessible. The task can then be tackled at a number of different levels. It is evident that there are some questions that are difficult to answer due to lack of information or disagreement between the sources. In order to write their accounts, pupils either need to reconcile these differences or use the language of uncertainty. The less able will be able to state which they think happened and which things they are certain of and which they are less certain of. Though they may not be able to articulate it yet they are being introduced to some of the issues of working with evidence. More able pupils will be able to explain how they reached decisions about particular events they put into their accounts.

The task is challenging, as pupils are working constructively with sources to build an account of an event from the past. But the way the task is set up allows all pupils to gain access at the 'ground floor', so they can all do something.

Figure 4.10 shows answers from two pupils. The first of these reports is from a pupil with particular problems relating to reading and writing. This piece of work represents a successful extended piece of writing for this pupil. He has stated what he thinks but has yet to explain how he reached his decisions. In

	Source 1	Source 2	Source 3	Source 4	Source 5
What colour was the scaffold?					
How many executioners were there?					
Were the executioners in disguise?					
Did the King have to lie, stoop or kneel down?					
Who helped tuck the King's hair in his cap?					
What signal did the King give to have his head cut off?					
How many blows did it take to cut off the King's head?					

Figure 4.9 Examining sources

discussion, he was able to present some basic reasons, mainly based around the idea of how frequently things were said or where there was little or no disagreement. The second answer is from a pupil generally considered to be below average ability. This time we can see there is a degree of reasoning behind some of the points he makes. In both cases, these answers represent a positive step forward for these pupils because they could access the material in the first place, the table helped them to structure their ideas, and they are starting to grapple more closely with how evidence can be used in a constructive manner to tell them something about the past.

The importance of contextual knowledge

Contextual knowledge is often taken for granted or watered down for pupils with special needs because it is thought that information overload can confuse

Primary sources

Source 1

Source 2

17-year-old Oxford undergraduate, Philip Henry,
actually saw the execution.

> *I stood amongst the crowd in the street before
> Whitehall Gate, and saw what was done, but was
> not so near as to hear anything. The blow I saw
> given, with a sad heart; at the instant whereof,
> there was such a groan by the thousands then
> present, as I may never hear again. There was,
> according to order, one troop immediately
> marching to Westminster and another from
> Westminster to confuse people, and to scatter
> them, so that I had much ado to escape home
> without hurt.*

Source 3

Source 4
The account of John Rushworth.

Then the king called Dr Juxon for his nightcap and having put it on, he said to the executioner, 'Does my hair trouble you?', who desired him to put it all under his cap, which the King did accordingly by the help of the executioner and the bishop.

Then the King took off his cloak and his George [i.e. the jewel showing St George, worn by Knights of the Garter] giving his George to Dr Juxon. After which the King stooping down, laid his neck upon the block. And after a little pause, stretching forth his hands, the executioner at one blow severed his head from his body.

Source 5
A foreign eyewitness quoted in M. Gibb, The Lord General.

On the scaffold, the king showed great courage. His beard was long and grey, his hair white and he was greatly aged. The two executioners were masked and wore false beards and wigs. Upon the scaffold were iron chains and ropes to allow force to be used with the king if he did not submit of his own accord to the axe.

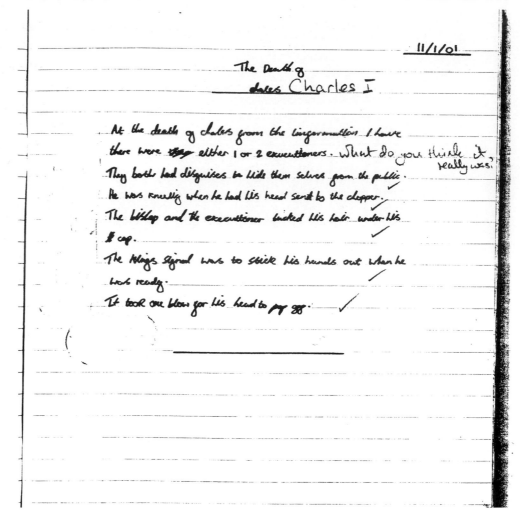

Figure 4.10 *Examples of pupils' reports when working with evidence*

them. This is an area that needs careful thought. Too much information can confuse pupils if given all at once. Too little information means they will be confused, as they haven't enough to make sense of the context. Consider the following commonly taught topic – the origins of the English Civil War. What challenges does this present?

- In terms of contextual knowledge, it needs some understanding of the development of Parliament under the Tudors and the subsequent difficulties James I faced.

- It requires an insight into systems of power and beliefs to comprehend ideas like 'Divine Right of Kings'.

- It needs understanding of specific terms such as 'Parliament', 'Puritan', 'power', and so on.

- It requires an understanding of causation – how causes can be grouped and linked together, and the relative importance of causes – all within the framework of the knowledge needed to comprehend the topic.

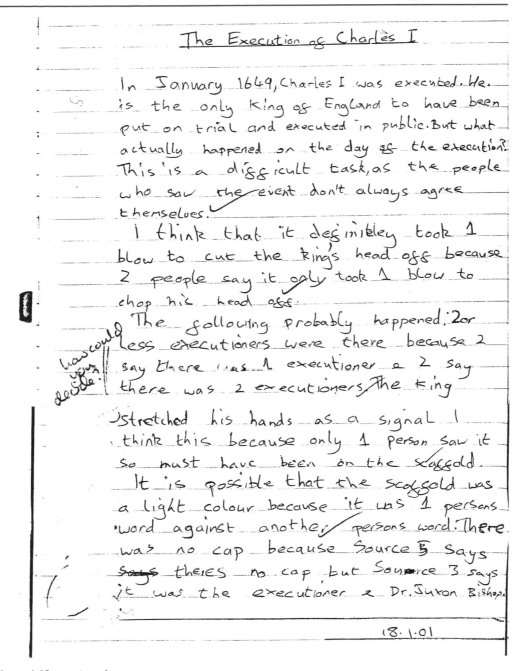

The Execution of Charles I

In January 1649, Charles I was executed. He is the only king of England to have been put on trial and executed in public. But what actually happened on the day of the execution? This is a difficult task, as the people who saw the event don't always agree themselves.

I think that it definitely took 1 blow to cut the king's head off because 2 people say it only took 1 blow to chop his head off.

The following probably happened: 2 or less executioners were there because 2 say there was 1 executioner & 2 say there was 2 executioners. The king stretched his hands as a signal. I think this because only 1 person saw it so must have been on the scaffold.

It is possible that the scaffold was a light colour because it was 1 persons word against another persons word. There was no cap because Source 5 says theres no cap, but Source 3 says it was the executioner & Dr. Juxon Bishop.

18.1.01

Figure 4.10 *continued*

Seen like this, the topic seems daunting. So how could we tackle this effectively and plan ways in for pupils? To engage the pupils, we could start at the end and tell a gripping tale of the execution of Charles I, but how do we deal with all the other issues raised above? The following is a suggestion:

- *Development of Parliament* – An overview could be created using a series of cards and a 'living graph'. Pupils have to position the cards in chronological order horizontally along the graph, but then place them vertically according to whether they show Parliament gaining more power or not.

- *Systems of power and beliefs* – Pupils can be reminded to consider the role and status of the king in medieval times, which they would have studied previously. Then, by referring back to the overview activity, they can see how this initial position was being threatened. A more in-depth study of the problems of James I could be undertaken. Use of both a depth and overview activity then provides a working contextual framework.

- *Understanding of specific terms* – Reference can be made to Parliament in the Middle Ages and its role, which can then be discussed further by referring to the overview work, so that pupils can see how the status of Parliament was starting to change. Reference to earlier work on religious changes under the Tudors and the religious problems of Elizabeth I can be used to remind pupils of the term 'Puritans' and what they stood for. These will help further boost the contextual framework, while getting pupils to reflect on the subject-specific language needed to tackle the work.

- *Causation* – Pupils can be warmed up to the idea of causation by considering earlier work that involved such ideas. (Can you think of other topics we have done that got us looking at why something happened? What did we learn from that about explaining why things happened, etc.)

INSET Activity

As a department, identify a topic that is complex for pupils. Identify what makes it a difficult topic – level of contextual knowledge, concepts, specific language, second order concepts? Identify what pupils should be able to draw on from prior work, and identify what new things need to be introduced to pupils. Devise a sequence of questions or tasks that will allow pupils to access this topic successfully.

Writing

Writing presents problems for many pupils, not just those with special needs. Why do pupils find writing difficult? Motivation is important and allowing the pupils to feel they can succeed is crucial. Essentially there are four key areas of difficulty:

- not understanding the topic;

- not understanding the task (a failure to understand the purpose of the writing);

- general difficulties with the writing process – handwriting, spelling;

- not being able to organise the piece of writing effectively.

Problems of understanding are partly due to the fragmentary nature of the curriculum. Pupils may only get an hour of history a week. For those with short memories this creates major obstacles, especially when a sequence of lessons is built around a topic. Lessons can too easily become compartmentalised, and pupils need to see how lessons link. This can partly be achieved by the use of 'big' questions or focus questions.

Figure 4.11 shows an example of a 'cunning plan' from *Teaching History*, where the big question drives the whole sequence of learning. Each lesson is

This unit contains complex concepts. It is distant from twentieth century life. The challenge is to understand power struggles between King and Parliament, a changing society and a religious upheaval. How do we interest students in religion when they live in a society in which religion takes a back seat?

Cunning Plan for Study Unit 3, "The Making of the United Kingdom 1500–1750"

It is by seeing the links between these areas that students will begin to understand the fabric of 16th and 17th century life. By blending big stories and little stories (or 'overview' and 'depth') we can overcome the complexity of the topic in a manner that gains interest and develops understanding. The overarching big question for Part 1 of the MUK workscheme is:

Why and with what consequences did Britain become a Protestant nation?

ENQUIRY 1
WHY DID THE KING'S GREAT MATTER MATTER?

Explain context: Henry VIII's marriage to Catherine of Aragon. Gain students' attention by using Henry's (saucy) love letters to Anne Boleyn:

…Mine own sweetheart, this shall be to advertise you of the great loveliness that I find here since your departing…Wishing myself in my sweetheart's arms, whose pretty dukkys (breasts) I trust shortly to kiss…

Students speculate and frame questions about the context and constraints around Henry's relationship with these women.

Link these to a series of problems that Henry might encounter. Get the pupils to understand the options open to Henry though:

- Writing reports by Henry's advisers on his problems;
- Classifying the options using cards;
- Doing mini-role plays;

By the end of these exercises (i) the story of the divorce will be clear; (ii) pupils' appetites will be whetted for more!

ENQUIRY 2
WHO CHANGED THINGS AND HOW?

Overview of Tudor religious change. Contrast church interiors. Students list *obvious* differences. Then help them to infer *fundamental* differences.

Include Edward VI, Mary and Elizabeth in your overview activities. Use simple tables. Illustrate with 'little' stories. By the end of this enquiry students will have a firm grasp of differences between Protestants and Catholics. We are now ready to explore the significance of these changes at a number of levels.

ENQUIRY 3
HOW DID RELIGIOUS CHANGES AFFECT ORDINARY PEOPLE?

Do this through 2 case studies:

(i) The motives and the impact of the dissolution of the monasteries. Build on Year 7 work on monasteries. For dramatic interest, start with the Pilgrimage of Grace.

(ii) Interpretations work on Mary: how did she get the nickname "Bloody"?

Start with Gunpowder Plot:

- Students sequence traditional story elements
- Place traditional story alongside new evidence. Students weigh new evidence and propose alternative explanations. Revisit, constantly, Enquiries 2 and 3 so that students understand *how* earlier developments shaped attitudes to the Catholics.

ENQUIRY 4
WHY DID ATTITUDES TOWARDS CATHOLICS HARDEN?

Now explain in outline the role of *religion* in Civil War and Glorious Revolution. Keep it lively. Emphasise Scotland's different experience. Let them see the story 'shape'. (This *introduces* religion's role in 17th century politics. Part 2 of work scheme will take King and Parliament as its theme.)

ENQUIRY 5
WHY AND WITH WHAT CONSEQUENCES DID BRITAIN BECOME A PROTESTANT NATION?

We're there! Now we can answer the big question. Teach students how to *apply* their knowledge to the question. For example, use 'evidence sandwiches' (see Margaret Mulholland in *Teaching History* Issue 91, May 1998). Pupils structure their writing around the ideas in Enquiries 1 to 4, thus shaping their own thoughtful, conceptually structured response to Enquiry 5.

Richard Harris
Kennet School (11–18 comprehensive) Berkshire

Figure 4.11 *A 'big' question driving the sequence of learning*

Teaching and Learning

related to the question in some way, though may focus on a range of historical issues. The key, though, is to get the pupils to keep making links between lessons. The use of formative assessment along the way also allows problems to be identified and remedied before the final piece of work is produced. This should allow pupils to be more confident in tackling work.

The purpose of writing has been addressed quite extensively within the literacy materials being produced by the DfES 2002. They identify eight categories of non-fiction writing: instructions, recount, explanation, information, persuasion, discursive, writing, analysis, and evaluation (see Figure 4.12).

At some point we may draw on all these styles of writing within history. The most common, though, are likely to be discursive, analytical, explanatory, evaluative and persuasive. These all need to be explained to the pupils so that they can understand the stylistic conventions of the piece of writing. For example, an answer looking at 'Why did the English Civil War break out in 1642?' will analyse a range of reasons, compare them, look at links between different ideas, present an argument, write in the past tense, and use connectives like 'this led to', 'this was important because', and so on.

This also links to the issue of organising the piece of writing, which presents problems in terms of selecting relevant material and deciding on the logical order in which to present it. The selection of material can be overcome by the use of content menus, sentence starters, scaffolding or writing frames that specifically focus pupils' attention on key pieces of information, as well as extensive discussion. Once the skeleton of an answer has been sketched out, the next hurdle is to get pupils to explain and elaborate upon the points they raise. Connectives can help prompt thinking, but modelling makes this more explicit. Pupils could be presented with a series of challenges here. The 'and so' challenge could get pupils to link pieces of information together. The 'because' challenge gets them to give a reason for something. The 'consequently' challenge gets pupils to give results of something. A range of such challenges could be devised, and would help all pupils in the class develop their thinking.

For some pupils, problems associated with writing are more severe. The process of making legible marks on the page, in straight lines and with correct spelling and punctuation can be a huge challenge. Where pupils have such difficulties, consult the SENCO for advice and appropriate materials. Where difficulties are severe, speech recognition software can be invaluable, a volunteer scribe can be drafted in, or the pupil can make an audio recording. For less severe difficulties consider:

- providing assorted pens/pencils with grips

- different types and colours of paper

- non-slip mats

- sloping desk tops

- a laptop computer – possibly with predictive software, or a PC with large format keyboard

- word banks

The categories as defined in the literacy strategy have clear limitations, as many overlap considerably, and one piece of writing may cover several categories at once. But what use do they have for thinking about history writing?

- *Instruction* – This has a few uses in history, though it is probably not the most common type of communication. However, it could be employed to get pupils to write manuals, for example describing the ways a medieval person could avoid catching the plague, or remedies to deal with the disease. It might usefully be employed for getting pupils to understand the processes involved in various aspects of history. Pupils might write guidance for each other about how to write an essay or how to analyse a source. Not only might this mean that such things are couched in pupil terms, it could also allow the teacher to understand what the pupils actually can and cannot do.

- *Recount* – This might be dismissed as the use of narrative, which many history teachers try to avoid. Yet, as discussed earlier, storytelling has a role to play within the history classroom, in particular because, for many pupils, a story approach helps them to understand better. The idea of getting pupils to write accounts of events can be a challenging yet accessible task, as illustrated by the example of the execution of Charles I mentioned earlier.

- *Explanation* – This is a key area within history. How did, or why did something happen are standard fare. As discussed in the chapter on monitoring and assessment, the degree of challenge from such tasks can vary considerably, depending on the particular question set.

- *Information* – Many non-historians might pigeonhole the subject as being about dates and facts. Therefore, information writing might be seen as the domain of the history department. This could take the form of compiling 'fact files' or profiles of key events or individuals, but this has the danger of degenerating into a copying exercise or a 'cut and paste' exercise from the Internet. Though this has some value, care must be taken to ensure that either the information gathered has had to be transformed prior to writing up or that, once the information has been found, it is used in a purposeful manner. For example, when studying the GCSE unit on the history of medicine, fact files could be created on key individuals such as Hippocrates, Galen, Vesalius, Pasteur, and so on. Once completed, the fact files could be used to evaluate the contribution of each individual, in order to decide who had the biggest impact on the development of medicine. Alternatively, pupils could be given a general information-gathering exercise, which could allow for gross copying of information from the Internet or CDRom, but once in class they could be forced to focus on something very specific. This has the advantage of being able to teach pupils how to track down the particular from a dense mass of 'stuff'.

- *Persuasion* – In essence, most essay writing is an attempt to present an opinion and persuade the reader that this opinion is valid. This style of writing could, however, be used in different contexts. For example, it could be used to prepare a speech justifying a point of view, such as the need for reform in nineteenth-century factories. These speeches could be presented either from the viewpoint of a contemporary or of a historian examining conditions with the benefit of hindsight.

- *Discursive writing, analysis and evaluation* – These later categories tend to offer the greatest chance of overlap. Questions that start 'To what extent . . .'; 'Why did x happen . . .'; 'How important was y . . .'; 'Which source would be most useful for . . .', and so on, offer the chance to discuss, analyse and evaluate issues. These qualities are often at the heart of most historical thinking and reasoning.

Figure 4.12 *The categories of non-fiction writing*

Being left-handed should not, in itself, constitute a difficulty, but such pupils will find it easier to work if they are not sitting next to a right-handed writer (they need space on their left side). Special scissors make cutting-out much easier.

Consider a 'finishing off' time for slower workers – a TA can supervise this session during a part of lunchtime, for example.

> ### INSET Activity
>
> *As a department, identify when pupils will have opportunities to write at length across a year or a key stage. What different sorts of writing will they undertake? What challenges will this writing present for different pupils? What steps can you take to help pupils develop their ability to write?*

Group work

Group work is often advocated as a means of helping pupils with special needs, either by grouping them with pupils of similar ability or in mixed groups where it is hoped that the more able will be able to model approaches to work, or help the less able make sense of the material. Group work, though, needs careful consideration if it is not to become a source of unfocused activity. Clarity of task is important in motivating pupils. Assigning specific roles to pupils is necessary to ensure they all have something to do. Time limits and providing sufficient time for the task are also needed. The time required will depend on the significance attached to the piece of work. For example, the pupils are set work on the Chartists. Their task is to find out whether they were successful and why. In order to do this they need to find out who the Chartists were, what they aimed to do, what they actually did and whether they were successful. Then they need to explore the reasons for their lack of success. To make the task more challenging, pupils could be asked to illustrate their talk with a number of sources and explain how these helped them answer the issues. There is, thus, a very clear set of objectives. If the class were to work in fours, one could be a chair, one could be the writer, one the reporter, and one the observer. Each role has a specific job description:

- *Role of the chair* – To organise the work of the group, to summarise at the end of the lesson what the group has achieved and what still needs to be done, to decide when one element of the work has been achieved so the group can focus on another task.

- *Role of the writer* – To produce the final written report for the group, to liaise with other members of the group to ascertain what they have found, and to help the chair decide when enough material has been found.

- *Role of the reporter* – To feed back the findings of the group to the class in whatever form is deemed appropriate.

- *Role of the observer* – To provide feedback to the teacher and the group on how well the group are working, identifying who has worked well and who has not, identifying factors that are helping the group to make progress or not. Their feedback provides important ideas about how the individuals can help groups work more effectively in the future.

Besides their general responsibility to help find out information to tackle the tasks, the pupils have very specific roles to help keep them focused. When circulating round groups it is then not only possible to ask about what they have found out, but also to see how well each is fulfilling their role. It is also a good idea for members of the group to have badges. This will help them, and you, remember who is supposed to be doing what. Initially, they will need to be trained to do the roles well, but with experience and debriefing about the way the groups have worked, they will become increasingly proficient in working in this manner.

Differentiation

Traditionally, differentiation in history has been seen as either the setting of the same work, using the same materials for all pupils, with outcome being the main form of differentiation, or differentiation by task, where the teacher has to create three different sets of materials, aimed at three different levels, essentially the creation of three lessons within one. Though these have their place, each has drawbacks.

The first means that some pupils will find the work too difficult and may become alienated. The second creates a lot of work for the teacher, and can inadvertently label pupils as the less able, because they get the 'easy' sheet. A simple way to avoid this last problem might be to ask pupils to choose the worksheet that challenges them most. However, as we have seen earlier, making the tasks accessible for all can circumvent many of these problems, allowing for meaningful differentiation by outcome and, therefore, not requiring the creation of three sets of work. However, there are other forms of differentiation that are useful:

- *By intervention* – This may be intervention by yourself or by a Teaching Assistant who has been primed to work with particular pupils. The intervention may be to clarify a piece of text or the demands of a task, so that pupils can continue with a task. At a more sophisticated level, it may require further explanation for a complex idea, using an analogy that would be familiar to the pupil, for example differences between communist and capitalist ideas.

- *By modification of materials* – This may be to provide a glossary with a piece of text to help pupils comprehend unusual words or phrases. It may well be to provide less information to prevent pupils being overwhelmed, particularly when working with a number of sources or cards for a sorting activity. This needs, however, to be handled carefully depending on the aims of the activity – providing too little information may actually make the task more unintelligible. For visually impaired pupils, it may mean the text enlarged on the photocopier.

- *By setting different expectations* – This can be particularly useful when a range of assessment criteria is clearly shared with the class. Pupils can be reminded about their previous work and be encouraged to maintain that standard of work or push further forward. This has the advantage of being individualised but without pupils feeling they have been 'ceilinged' in what they can achieve.

- *By scaffolding* – This is where a task is broken down into a series of more manageable steps. This could be within a lesson or across a series of lessons where the product of the lesson will eventually form a bigger piece of work. Care needs to be taken that pupils are not restricted in what they can ultimately achieve. Writing frames are often a useful way of scaffolding a piece of written work, but if they are overly prescriptive in what pupils have to say, they can automatically hold some children back. For example, when doing some work on the question, 'Why and with what consequences did Britain become a Protestant nation?', I provided all pupils with a 'big' and 'little' point form of scaffolding (see Figure 4.24 below). Pupils had to arrange the 'big' points into a logical order, and then put relevant 'little' points that supported the 'big' points. Pupils did this quite happily and it did allow all pupils to see how to construct a piece of writing. But many pupils were unwilling to explain more fully the significance of the points they had put together. It also constrained those who were capable of explaining their ideas properly. The exercise worked better when, after the initial sorting, pupils had to explain orally what they had put together, and could be prompted to explain further.

    In addition, some pupils might benefit from only being given the 'big' points and be challenged to find their own supporting 'little' points. The exercise could even be broken down further by separating the question into its two components of 'why' and 'with what consequences' for pupils to work on.

- *By question* – As mentioned earlier, questioning is important in helping pupils progress and can be differentiated. Don't, however, simply restrict factual recall or comprehension questions to weaker pupils, as this will not help them develop their understanding of a topic. The way a question is phrased can alter the level of challenge, e.g. 'Why was there a revolution in France in 1789?' is a less challenging question in many ways than 'To what extent was Louis XVI responsible for the French Revolution?'

    Obviously, the first question could be asked of a Year 7 pupil, as well as a history professor, with different results. The first question allows for an explanation of a range of factors that may result in a discussion of one or of several valid reasons, but all pupils should be able to offer something. The second question demands a judgement, weighing the importance of one reason against others. This is more difficult to handle. There is no reason why different questions could not be set around a topic that has been taught to all pupils in the class, if it is going to allow pupils to achieve something worthwhile.

- *By task* – A suggested approach is to present pupils with a range of activities set out in a grid, with pupils having to complete a row of tasks (see Figure 4.13 below). This allows you to set up tasks of varying difficulty in different ways, so that pupils can either choose or be directed towards particular rows.

Big points

An important consequence was that Catholics became very unpopular.

The main reason for the change to Protestantism was Henry VIII's divorce.

In the long term, the Protestant religion only became accepted under Elizabeth I, partly due to her own popularity.

In the short term, in the 1530s, 1540s and 1550s, there was a lot of unrest caused by the religious changes.

Little points

Henry VIII wanted a son to succeed him.

Henry VIII's marriages left three children: Mary who was Catholic; Edward and Elizabeth who were Protestant.

Figure 4.13 *Big points and little points*

This is a photocopiable exercise.

Elizabeth became very popular after the defeat of the Spanish Armada in 1588.

Henry VIII closed down all the monasteries in the 1530s and 1540s.

Henry VIII had fallen in love with Anne Boleyn.

Henry VIII thought God might be punishing him for marrying his dead brother's wife.

Closing the monasteries angered many ordinary people and led to a rebellion called the Pilgrimage of Grace.

The Gunpowder Plot was used by Robert Cecil to frame the Catholics.

Elizabeth I followed a moderate religious policy. This tried to keep both Protestants and Catholics happy.

Henry VIII thought controlling the Church would give him more power and money.

Both Edward VI and Mary faced rebellions from people who did not like their religious changes.

Elizabeth I carefully tried to make herself popular. This can be seen in her portraits.

Queen Mary killed 284 Protestants who refused to become Catholic.

Figure 4.13 *continued*

This is a photocopiable exercise.

	A	B	C
1	Why did William the Conqueror win the Battle of Hastings?	Using worksheet A, put the pictures from the Bayeaux Tapestry into order to tell the story of 1066.	Explain why William invaded England in 1066.
2	Draw/copy a map of England. Mark on Harold's movements for 1066. How does this help explain his defeat?	Look at sources A and B. How do they say Harold died?	What was the most important reason why William won the Battle of Hastings? Give a reason for your answer.
3	Which is the better source for finding out about the Battle of Hastings – the Bayeaux Tapestry or William of Poitiers?	Why did Harold lose the Battle of Hastings?	Using worksheet B, sort the written extracts into order to tell the story of the Battle of Hastings.

Figure 4.14 A task grid

The grid contains written work (which can be differentiated in a number of ways), and some visual work, and it focuses on the story of 1066, as well as developing pupils' ability to reason and explain, and work with sources. The tasks all present differing degrees of difficulty. This resource is obviously very flexible in how it could be used.

Homework

If we wish to encourage pupils to work well, away from the classroom, they need to be set activities that are accessible and manageable, and that they will want to do. Account should be taken of preferred learning styles just as in the classroom.

Consider work on the Great Fire of London. Pupils have been studying the question 'Why did the Great Fire of London cause so much damage?' In class, the pupils were hooked in by the contrast between the teacher's account of the fire and Pepys' nonchalant diary entry where he notices the fire then goes back to bed! The drama of the event was brought out via contemporary paintings and a map showing the extent of the damage. Pupils then speculated as to why the fire might have caused so much damage.

This was then followed up by a card-sort exercise where pupils examined different causes and sorted them, firstly by long to short term, then categorised them under headings, and finally discussed which were the more important reasons. The class was then debriefed about which way of sorting was easiest, which was most difficult, and why. There was a general discussion about issues surrounding causal reasoning.

What would be a suitable homework to consolidate this lesson? It needs pupils to demonstrate their understanding of causation – for some it may be to give a simple or a few simple reasons, for others it may be to explain their reasoning, or even to show how the different reasons are linked.

More departments are now allowing pupils choice over the way work is presented as long as it meets the required learning objectives. Taking the example above, the following tasks could be offered to a class:

- Draw/copy and label a map of London, indicating reasons for the extent of the damage (some pupils might even wish to create a model).

- Create a causation diagram, where causes are colour coded (e.g. long/short term, under different categories, most/least important), with arrows showing links between factors.

- Create a storyboard of the Great Fire, which highlights the key reasons for the damage caused.

- Have a worksheet with different reasons already laid out around the edge of the page. Pupils have to draw arrows between factors that are connected. Pupils have to number the factors in order of importance. Pupils have to explain (orally or in writing) why they have linked one pair of factors together, and why they have chosen a factor as the most important.

- Create a role play, where pupils in groups have to script a court of inquiry, examining the reasons for the amount of damage caused.

- Write an essay.

- Create a tape/video recording explaining why the fire caused so much damage.

- Create a PowerPoint presentation explaining why the fire caused so much damage.

- Complete a cloze exercise

Each task presents different degrees of challenge to pupils but, given a choice, pupils can opt for a task that best suits their ability, but which should enable the teacher a good insight into that child's level of understanding. Think about a class you teach – which of these activities would they be able to do and would want to do?

Part of the challenge is to provide work for those children where there may be problems that make working at home difficult, and tasks that can be completed by the child without teacher support, though obviously if there is a school homework club this could be used. (If this is to be used it is always a good idea to give whoever runs the club an idea of the work to be done so they can be more effective.) Alternatively, a departmental homework club or history club could be used to offer more support for pupils. Looking at the list of tasks set out for the Great Fire of London, consider which ones will require support, which can be easily done by the child on their own, how long each task might take, and what facilities would be needed to complete them.

INSET Activity

As a department, discuss a topic you all teach, identify the learning objectives and then come up with at least three different homework activities that would meet them. Include activities that need varying degrees of support. Having worked on one together, designate individuals to create similar alternatives for other topics.

Planning a lesson

The essentials here are what you want the pupils to learn, how they are going to learn it, and how you will know they have learnt it! This is all standard fare for good teachers, but pupils with special needs can be helped by greater awareness of what is going to happen in the lesson. For example, I had a student with ADHD who was very disruptive in lessons. A TA noticed that one of his most frequent requests concerned time – 'What is the time?', 'How long is left in the lesson?' and so on. As a result, I started to provide him with an outline of the lesson, indicating what was going to be done, and when, and how long I expected each activity to last. As we went through the lesson, he could tick off things as they were done, and seemed far more settled after that. It seemed that once he had a sense of where the lesson was going, how much was left to do, and how long things were going to last for, he could focus more easily.

This emphasises the need for all pupils to be aware of what is going to happen in terms of learning objectives, how they will be met and what, therefore, pupils can expect to learn in the lesson, or even sequence of lessons. Putting lesson plans onto OHTs can easily meet these needs or, as indicated, a personal outline for someone can be very helpful.

It is also important to be aware here of pupils with IEPs and their particular targets. Their needs ought to be addressed within lesson planning. It may be appropriate to provide some form of differentiated material, but it may be something like ensuring they participate within the lesson orally or write using full stops and capital letters (see section on 'Managing Support' for further advice).

CHAPTER 5

Inclusive Classrooms

The classroom environment

The classroom environment is an important consideration for all pupils. This includes the physical environment, the emotional needs of the class and the creation of a culture of learning.

The physical environment

The layout of the room is important for some pupils purely as regards means of access – both wheelchair users and pupils with visual impairment need to feel welcome, and any difficulties when getting to a place send out the wrong messages to them. It is also important to think about maintaining space for them to get out of the class while the lesson is in progress, such as to use the toilet (and when they are new to a classroom, remember to ensure that they know how they can get out and where the necessary facilities are). Routines about where coats and bags are placed need to be enforced in order to allow easy access.

It is also necessary to check the visibility of the board from different angles of the room. Is it clearly visible? Is there any glare from the whiteboard caused by lighting or windows? Is the teacher's desk in front of the board, in which case you may be obscuring someone's view? Considerations like these can make a significant difference to particular pupils.

Deciding where to seat pupils can affect their performance in the classroom. Pupils with VI clearly need to be near the board and where there is good lighting. Pupils with hearing impairment need to be seated away from things that might create a background hum, like OHPs and some heaters. They also need to be seated where there is good lighting, as people's facial expressions are often used as a clue when listening to someone speak. Pupils with Asperger's ought to be asked where best they would like to sit, as they often need personal space and may need to sit at the end of a row. Additionally, some pupils with this condition find strip lighting in class a distraction and need to sit near natural light. It is best to discuss seating with these pupils as each individual can have very different problems. Pupils with ADHD need to sit away from distractions as far as possible – sitting them next to the video or bookcase will give them lots of things to fiddle with during the course of a lesson! If they are right (left) handed it is often a good idea to sit them near the front, on the left (right) hand side of the room as this makes it more awkward for them to turn around and face the rest of the pupils in the class.

For many pupils, not just those with SEN, school chairs are extremely uncomfortable, especially when you consider pupils are often required to sit quietly in them for up to an hour or more at a time. It is possible to get chairs that offer more posture support, which is particularly important for those who are not always confined to their wheelchair. They need the extra support such chairs can offer. Consult with the SENCO and/or OT for advice and information about availability. It may well help to include some physical activity within the lesson to allow pupils the chance to move around.

Displays are encouraged, and rightly so, in the classroom. Careful thought needs to be given, though, to how these are arranged. Too much information in one space can overload some pupils. A dazzling array of colour, mixing in pupils' work with key words and phrases that pupils might use, may look nice, but will be of little benefit to someone with a visual impairment or Asperger's or ADHD. Displays ought to be clearly demarcated and labelled so that pupils' attention can focus on one thing at a time.

Similarly, teachers need to think about how they use the board in the classroom. It is important to consolidate ideas and, to break instructions down into simple steps for pupils to follow, but, again, too much information can confuse some pupils and they will be unable to concentrate properly. Avoid the need for copying lots of information from the board as this can be difficult for many pupils; if the information is needed for future reference then give pupils a photocopied sheet or use different coloured board pens for alternate lines as this will make it easier to follow. Different colours are also useful for highlighting important pieces of information or showing groups of ideas on the board, such as instructions for the lesson, learning objectives, answers the pupils provide during discussion, and so on. The use of interactive whiteboards can be extremely useful in this respect. Notes you make on the board can be saved as you go through the lesson – after the lesson these can either be printed out for pupils with particular needs or saved onto the school network for future reference.

Teachers also need to consider where they place themselves in the classroom when addressing the class. Being silhouetted against a window will make it difficult for pupils with hearing and visual impairments to make sense of what you are saying, as they often need facial expressions to help them. Body language and tone of voice are also important clues for some pupils, so consideration needs to be given to these as well.

In addition, there is a range of technology that can be utilised within the classroom to aid pupils – magnifiers for the visually impaired, word processors or laptops for those who have problems with writing skills, and audio equipment for pupils to listen to work or record their work. Consult with the

SENCO about this sort of equipment – it can often be borrowed from the LEA support service, a local support group or national charity at little or no cost to the school.

The emotional needs of the class

Teaching may be many things but it is never boring – because every class is unique. Two classes of nominally the same ability classification will never display the same strengths and weaknesses when approaching a topic or developing a skill. Extended writing tasks that caught the imagination of a class one year cannot be guaranteed to succeed to the same degree if attempted again. Discussions that stimulated, provoked, stretched and amused once may barely spark at all with a different set of youngsters. Such is the challenge of teaching, and such is its beauty. There is never room for complacency, and lesson ideas must constantly evolve as the needs, likes, strengths and weaknesses of every class are taken into account.

So what is a 'class'? Clearly it is a collection of individuals, each with his or her unique educational needs – some with educational needs that are considered 'special' in some way – and each with his or her own individual emotions and personality. But can a 'class' really have its own collective needs? Yes, in the sense that the needs of the class as a whole are a result of the combination and interaction of the educational needs, emotions and personality of the individuals within that class.

The recognition by the teacher that a class has collective needs is vital if the individuals within it are to fulfil their individual learning potential. Of these collective needs, emotional needs command particular attention if effective learning is to take place because, if emotional needs are addressed, then the class as a whole will move towards the ideal learning state of 'relaxed alertness' as defined by Hughes 1999. As Hughes 1999: 25 states: 'Pupils do not learn effectively when placed under negative stress', yet negative stress is exactly what will be generated if the emotional needs of a class are not addressed. Similarly, a teacher teaches most effectively when he or she is relaxed – and the effective consideration of the emotional needs of the class is a pre-requisite if such relaxation is to be possible.

What, then, *are* the emotional needs of the class and, just as importantly, how are they to be addressed?

- *The Need for confidence* – Pupil confidence is a precious commodity indeed. Collective and individual confidence must be carefully instilled and constantly nurtured in a class. Confidence is both the ignition for, and the accelerator of, success. A class that believes in its own capacity for success will rise to every new challenge with optimism, and will view setbacks as minor hiccoughs rather than insurmountable obstacles. A youngster with special needs will feed from this collective class confidence, providing that his or her needs have been taken into account in planning for a truly inclusive classroom, as described elsewhere in this chapter. Confidence can be effectively boosted by *constant declaration by the teacher of faith in a class's ability* to tackle a given task, coupled with acknowledgement that the task does present some challenge, e.g. 'This will not be easy but I know that this class can cope'. The acknowledgement of challenge is crucial in order that, in the event of difficulty, the class will see such as a consequence of the complexity of the task, not as collective or individual failure. This technique not only boosts the youngsters' confidence but also increases their self-esteem by asserting the teacher's faith in them collectively. The same techniques can be used with individual pupils by both the teacher and TAs. Of course, it is essential that the level of challenge *is* appropriate!

- *The need to treat a class with respect* – even during the trying times. Always take the tone that excessive noise, failure to concentrate, etc. is wrong because the class has allowed itself to divert from its usual high standards.

- *The need to show concern, patience, kindness and a willingness to help* – but *never* trying to be the friend of the class. You will always be their teacher, and their dignity and yours is best preserved by remembering that. There will be times when reprimands – on the terms above – are necessary, and these carry no weight from a 'mate' of equal status. Equally, praise is more effective from a concerned adult who has earned respect.

- *The need to give well-earned praise at the appropriate level* – Do not use 'excellent' as an entry term of praise, as this will quickly be devalued. Use a range of praise: 'good try', 'well done', 'good work', 'super', 'a real improvement', 'well-thought-out'. Above all, though, be sure only to praise real effort. Never use praise as a form of appeasement and (at least publicly) use the same forms of praise for all. It may well be an achievement for a child with Tourette's to avoid spitting or swearing for part of a lesson, but if praise for this is uttered aloud it may give the class as a whole a distorted sense of value. Praise in avoiding negative behaviour associated with certain syndromes is best uttered in the achieving child's ear. This will best serve the needs of both class and individual. Just as importantly, never use false praise as appeasement for a child. The value of real praise from you will be undermined forever in the eyes of the class and in the eyes of the child you are seeking to appease. Praise should be given either when a child knows that he or she has done well – in which case it becomes a reward. Or praise should be applied when a child is in doubt as to whether the work is 'any good' – here it is a confidence tool, building for the future.

- *The need to defuse the frustration of impatience* – Youngsters waiting for help while a teacher is helping another pupil – particularly those with ADHD or Asperger's – can quickly boil over into rage or drastic action to gain the teacher's attention. The chances of this can be greatly reduced by the simple expedient of acquiring the habit of looking up from helping a pupil from time to time, spotting the hands raised and allocating an order of attention by saying aloud: 'I'll come to Kuni next, then Sally, then Alistair'. You won't always get the order correct, but the pupils will see that you are attempting to be fair and, most importantly, they will know that they have been seen, and that waiting may not be indefinite. Also when questioning a class orally, don't allow 'callers out' to jump the queue of those waiting to answer. Insist on a hand up and come back to the caller out when he or she has complied. This may well cause a difficult situation the first time, but in the long run a damaging perception of unfairness, with associated disillusionment, will have been avoided. Any pupil with a syndrome making it difficult for them to wait a turn to answer will need the support and encouragement of a TA during Q & A sessions if this technique is to be used to maximum effect.

- *Awareness of the sensitivities of pupils* – Teenagers are easily embarrassed at the best of times and will frequently try to cover embarrassment with disruptive or loud behaviour. Use the expertise of your TA to discuss the sensitivities of individual pupils. Some may detest answering aloud and may need to be coaxed into it by offering a previously discussed and approved answer. Picking 'cold' on such a child to offer an answer aloud – even with a genuine intention of encouragement – could lead to a disastrous loss of confidence. Some may love reading work out but will never volunteer. Some may be uncomfortable with written answers but thrive in debate. Calling upon the strengths of pupils at an appropriate time can lead to an atmosphere of thriving success within a class. Touching on the sore points of weakness can destroy collective learning just as surely.

- *Treat youngsters with SEN as a true part of a class not as an adjunct to it.* This is the greatest emotional need of all in forging a true class team spirit. Set out with this intention and it will happen to the benefit of all. Regard SEN pupils as an obstacle to the learning of the rest of the class and just as surely all will suffer as pupils pick up very quickly on the attitude of a teacher. This is the essence of true inclusion – the teaching of a class as well as the individuals in that class: a grand aim but achievable in small, significant steps. It can be compared to building a cathedral brick by brick. It is worth remembering that little things mean a lot:

  – Even when a TA is working one to one with a pupil still show appreciation of that pupil's work by looking closely and offering praise and/or advice.

  – Show willingness to wait for an answer.

  – Offer a smile in reaction to effort.

  – Make eye-contact possible.

  – Try to avoid allowing a child with SEN to work to different learning objectives, even when learning activities are different by necessity.

  – Use differentiation with sensitivity, offering choice of activity where possible.

Remember: Human beings are creatures of function and emotion. Success in the functions of the educational process for all children rests upon 'relaxed alertness' (Hughes, 1999: 25). Relaxed alertness comes from awareness of the emotional needs of the class.

Creating a learning culture

Classrooms can be a confusing place for many pupils. Not only are they trying to master a range of different subjects, but also they have to deal with numerous teachers who each have peculiar ways of operating and different rules they enforce in their classroom. Staff need to refer to school policies and rules and try to be consistent in upholding them. At the very least, rules need to be consistently adhered to within a classroom.

But what rules are necessary to achieve this, and are easy to implement consistently and clearly understood by pupils? It would be easy to come up with a long list of things, but they would get forgotten and so become a source of conflict. Often such lists are prefixed with the word 'don't' which generates a negative feel as well. I prefer to use a simpler system based on three rights. This has the benefit of being easy to remember, and it has the advantage that pupils have two rights as opposed to the teacher who has one right! These are:

- The teacher has a right to teach without being disturbed in the process.

- The pupils have the right to learn without being disturbed in the process.

- Pupils have the right to be stuck.

The first two have the advantage of being vague enough to be useful – pupils generally know if they are getting in the way of teachers teaching and learners learning. For those who may not, such as pupils with Autistic Spectrum Disorders, then it is important that the inappropriateness of their behaviour is carefully explained to them. However, these rights can be further exemplified on a separate poster, as shown below.

Allowing the teacher to teach means:

- You have to keep quiet and pay attention when I speak.
- You have to put up a hand and wait before making a comment or asking a question.
- You have to become silent when I ask for quiet.

Allowing pupils to learn means:

- When working individually do not speak to the person/people sitting near to you.
- Do not 'borrow' things without the permission of the person they belong to.
- Do not call out for someone's attention – raise your hand and wait for the teacher.

The right to be stuck means:

- If you do not understand something, please put up your hand and wait for the teacher to help you.

The teacher also needs to remember to model the behaviours they want, as this helps set the tone of the classroom – e.g. when a class is concentrating and working quietly, it is often the teacher who breaks the silence. Of course, this may be necessary, but not in all cases.

In my experience, the final right is the most important in encouraging a more open dialogue between pupils and teacher. We need to encourage 'stuckness' and celebrate it, as it is an opportunity to learn. Pupils need to feel they can ask for clarification without feeling silly or stupid. In my class we will often stop and applaud someone who is stuck to reinforce the idea of its value.

Using ICT in history lessons

The evidence suggests that the use of ICT within history is patchy. But in terms of pupils with SEN does it have a role to play? The answer depends entirely on whether it is an appropriate way to learn history. For most pupils, getting them to type up neat answers on computers is essentially a waste of time, unless of course a pupil has a problem physically writing. ICT is useful where it helps historical thinking and makes the processing of historical information easier.

It is important, though, to consider whether ICT will actually add an extra barrier to learning. If pupils have to produce a multimedia presentation, the complexities of ICT can get in the way of learning history. I am, however, a great fan of using basic computer facilities because they can help with some big thinking!

Take the humble word processor. BECTa have produced some very simple but powerful materials for use in the classroom. Using the cut and paste function, putting text into italics, emboldening or underlining text, pupils have to manipulate text in many different ways. Reading a passage of text, pupils could take some headings that summarise the paragraph and paste them next to the appropriate paragraph. Using bold or underlining, the difference between fact and opinion can be highlighted in the text. Timelines can be made by cutting and pasting material into boxes to create a sequence of events.

The beauty of such an approach is that it avoids the mechanics of writing that can deter some pupils, and simply allows them to think about what is in front of them. If it goes wrong, the undo button on a word-processing package is marvellous! It allows pupils to experiment without penalty. Figure 5.1 (below) shows part of one of these activities. The headings in Table 1A need to be matched to appropriate paragraphs in a page of text, while Table 2A requires pupils to start selecting causes from the text and pasting them into the table. It allows pupils to concentrate on thinking about the history concepts, in this case causation, without having to worry over the obstacle of writing or getting it wrong. It also helps to develop literacy skills and hopefully boosts the confidence of pupils. Some activities are easily adaptable. Trainees of mine have developed similar exercises for a wide range of topics, from slavery to the Restoration, the murder of Becket to the impact of World War II.

PowerPoint is another simple package that can allow good historical thinking

Key question: Why was William able to defeat Harold Godwinson in 1066?

Task 1 What happened?

Table 1A

William lands in England

William crowned King of England

Battle of Hastings

Harold marches to meet William

Three claims but only one throne

Harold's difficult position

Harold Godwinson attacks Harold Hardrada

William's plans for invasion

Task 2 Why did it happen?

Table 2A

	Why did Harold lose the struggle for the English throne in 1066?
Cause A	
Cause B	
Cause C	
Cause D	
Cause E	
Cause F	

Figure 5.1 *Manipulating text on a computer*

to be developed. It is ideally suited for handling visual images and doing a 'layers of inference' approach. Having the same picture on a sequence of slides, allows pupils to focus firstly on what is actually in the picture, then to put their inferences onto a second slide and then the sort of questions that the picture raises on a final slide. Alternatively, difficult images can be easily tackled. Pupils could label a slide with all the things they don't understand, which the teacher could then answer, thereby allowing pupils to finish with a caption that summarises the meaning of the image. The slide sorter facility of PowerPoint allows for images to be chronologically sequenced. For example, different portraits of Elizabeth 1 could be jumbled up, and with some research or ready-made captions, pupils could put them into chronological order. They could then look at them as a set and identify ways the pictures change and don't change.

This could create some interesting questions about why Elizabeth doesn't seem to get any older once she is queen, which in turn could lead into ideas about the purpose and nature of images as propaganda.

Spreadsheets and databases offer ways of handling large quantities of information that would be impossible to use otherwise, and allow patterns to emerge in the past and generate questions. Again, BECTa have produced some valuable material here. For example, a database of around 400 castles allows for some excellent work to happen. The database can be searched by century to identify when castles were built – the peaks in building activity obviously generate the question as to why it happened at that time, and this could lead into further research. Looking at where castles were built is interesting and, again, when combined with questions about when, allows patterns of activity to be identified in the past.

A common problem with the use of the Internet is that pupils tend to accept whatever they read as true. They use it uncritically as a mine of information. This can be used to our advantage by picking out sites that are contradictory or go against what the pupils know. For example, work on King John or Richard III would produce a range of very different sites, both in terms of type of site and what they actually say. Using a series of structured points about who has produced the site, why, what they say and so on, will get pupils to see that different interpretations exist on the Internet. Not only does this hopefully get them thinking more critically about the World Wide Web, but it is also getting them to develop some complex, yet crucial insights into the workings of history. One major problem with the Internet is the volume of material available. Some pupils will easily get lost in the mass of information and become disheartened. It is important, therefore, to start building up a bank of suitable sites, and either have these set up on the school's intranet or have sites hyperlinked to worksheets on the school system. If time is an issue, then start small, identifying a few sites for a particular topic, or even get some pupils in a history club to surf the web for you and provide you with a summary of ten sites you might consider using.

For some pupils, simulations on computers can be useful in exploring what actually happened. The BBC website has a growing number of simulation activities for topics such as the Battle of Hastings, where pupils can make decisions and see what happens as a result. This can help them to see the importance of particular factors.

A new development that offers great potential is the use of interactive whiteboards. They cater particularly for visual and kinaesthetic learning to happen but, by using the full multi-media capabilities of the technology, auditory learners can also benefit. In addition, using an interactive whiteboard should help a teacher make sounder judgements about the level of understanding within a lesson, as pupils can be encouraged to come up and do things on the whiteboard, which allows for immediate feedback. If pupils cannot physically get up to the whiteboard to do things, they could use a laptop, which would allow those with physical disabilities to participate actively as well.

In terms of text-based work, the teacher can use a whiteboard to record ideas,

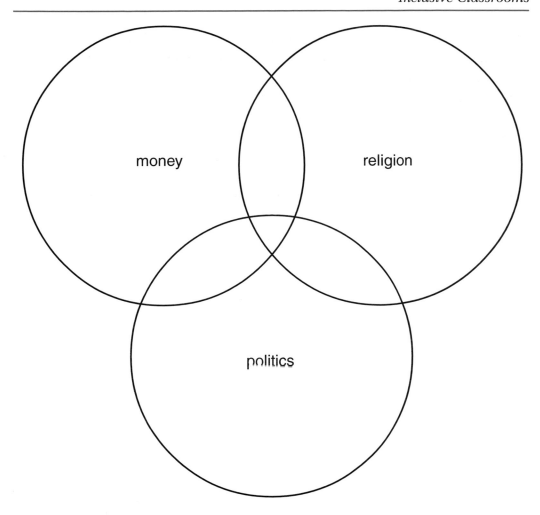

sort information, or to annotate material. As ideas are recorded on the board during a brainstorming session, these can then be grouped. For example, you might start a lesson by recapping key points of the Treaty of Versailles, which could then be put into groups such as land, armaments, and so on. Using pre-prepared text you could do a sorting exercise. Causes of the English Civil War could be sorted, using a Venn diagram, into categories to do with money, religion and politics. Pupils could be asked to come up to the board and physically move the different reasons and place them on the diagram, thus allowing the teacher to gauge their understanding. A pre-prepared piece of text could be annotated to pick out particular language or to identify certain facts or opinions or the tone of a source. For example, Figure 5.2 is an extract from Dickens' novel *Bleak House*. It is a wonderfully rich description of slum dwellings, which many might shy away from using with pupils with special needs. However, the question is: why would you want pupils to read such a piece of text? To extract information about the problems of slum dwellings might be possible, but then this might not be the best source of information. If, however, you wanted to pick out what Dickens was saying and how, then identifying the tone of the source would be very valuable. Figure 5.3 provides a possible word bank for pupils to draw on. They could identify different tones within the text and highlight them on the board which would in turn help them to understand Dickens' message, and lead into a discussion of what he was trying to achieve and why.

Jo lives – that is to say, Jo has not yet died – in a ruinous place, known to the like of him by the name of Tom-all-Alone's. It is a bleak, dilapidated street avoided by all decent people; where the crazy houses were seized upon, when their decay was far advanced, by some bold vagrants, who, after establishing their own possession, took to letting them out in lodgings.

Now these tumbling tenements contain, by night, a swarm of misery. As on the ruined human wretch, vermin parasites appear, so, these ruined shelters have bred a crowd of foul existence that crawls in and out of gaps in walls and boards; and coils itself to sleep in maggot numbers, where the rain drips in; and comes and goes, fetching and carrying fever, and sowing more evil in its every footprint than Lord Coodle and Sir Thomas Doodle, and the Duke of Foodle, and all the fine gentlemen in office, down to Zoodle, shall set right in five hundred years.

Twice, lately, there has been a crash and a cloud of dust, like the springing of a mine in Tom-all-Alone's; and each time, a house has fallen. These accidents have made a paragraph in the newspapers, and have filled a bed or two in the nearest hospital. The gaps remain, and there are not unpopular lodgings among the rubbish. As several more houses are nearly ready to go, the next crash in Tom-all-Alone's may be expected to be a good one.

Comments
This extract is from Charles Dickens' novel *Bleak House*, written in 1853. Dickens was concerned about the welfare of the poor and often tried to shock his readers. His work is therefore prone to exaggeration but is often based on personal experience or things he had knowledge of.

Figure 5.2 *Extract from* Bleak House

Which of these words describe the tone in Dickens' description?
What other words can you think of to use?

ridiculing

angry

honest

ironic

happy   sarcastic

sad

nervous   cross

flippant

humorous

Figure 5.3 *Word bank*

In terms of visual material, either still pictures or film can be watched and annotated. A layers of inference approach could be used when examining cartoon sources or portraits, while the use of the video player function on the latest version of Smart Board software allows you to view DVD material, pause the film, annotate the scene, save it to a notebook, and then watch further footage. By repeating this a few times, you could carefully analyse how particular scenes portray characters or events. This can make quite complex information more easily accessible, as it is possible to work together as a class to deconstruct something like Laurence Olivier's portrayal of Richard III, and compare it to Ian McKellan's interpretation. Similarly, material from the Internet can be viewed, annotated and copied, so the Richard III's Society website could be seen and contrasted with the information gained from work done on the film versions of Richard III.

Essentially, the key approach with ICT is to start with something manageable that develops historical understanding. This can then be repeated or adapted to bring in greater difficulty, once pupils have mastered both the ICT component and the historical thinking required. It is also very important that there is good liaison between history and ICT departments. Does the ICT co-ordinator understand what is needed in a history context? For example, it took me a long time to convince the ICT co-ordinator that PowerPoint would be a valuable tool for doing history. Similarly, are you aware of how pupils are taught to use the Internet in ICT? This might be of use so that you know how to teach pupils to interrogate the Web.

Final thoughts

Teaching is a complex business and teachers can often be overwhelmed by initiatives and ideas. The ideas contained in this chapter and the previous one would be difficult to implement simultaneously. We do, however, suggest that you make appropriate moves towards helping pupils with special needs more systematically. Start with ideas that appeal and seem manageable, and deliberately, over a period of time, build these into your practice. We have often found that by using ideas like those discussed above, all pupils, not just those with SEN, prosper. The most important thing, though, is that pupils with SEN can participate and move forward.

CHAPTER 6

Role Play and Practical Demonstration: a Route to Historical Causation, Concepts and Context

Let us first define what role play must *not* be if it is to serve all our pupils well: it must not be an elaborate play based on pages of inflexible script delivered by a minority of the class to a baffled and rarely silent majority. The picture conjured up here is one of mumbled lines and mangled vocabulary which serves only to obscure the true learning objectives of the lesson. This model of role play will actually work *against* inclusion, as pupils not involved in the main speaking parts and unable to maintain concentration in the face of their classmates' reading of a script, will quickly become detached and disaffected. Equally, it will destroy the confidence of any special needs pupil who will certainly blame him or herself for being unable to follow the course of the lesson.

Yet, by following a few simple rules, role play and its closely associated technique of practical demonstration (whereby pupils become the active demonstration model to illustrate difficult concepts), can offer a route towards viewing history from within. The personal experience offered by these techniques can become the key with which to provide access to the past and to the study of the past. These techniques are hugely powerful tools for inclusion and are particularly effective in addressing the needs of both the natural kinaesthetic learner and of those who have become kinaesthetic learners by default, through lack of success with traditional visual and auditory methods.

The rules for successful role play

1 *The vast majority of the class must be involved in the activity to some degree.*
   This involvement can be as little as hissing Charles on his entrance and exit in the trial role play exemplified below. Polite applause at pre-ordained times – as a member of the democratic parties in the Reichstag activity, for example, will also suffice to make the shyer members of any class experience a degree of empathy, and may well pave the way for greater involvement later in the year.

2 *The role play must be simple enough to be performable with no rehearsal.* Short, sharp activities work best. These lay one concept or idea bare and leave the class keen and wanting more.

3 *Speaking parts should be confined to one or two lines and should not demand advanced reading skills.* Complex scripts distort meaning and message when read aloud tortuously. They are also a barrier to inclusive practice.

4 *Follow-up should be immediate while the excitement and motivation of the activity is fresh in pupils' minds.* Debrief in role is particularly effective. 'And why, King Charles, did your trial seem so unfair?' 'Did it seem unfair to you, Bradshaw?' 'Why did you hiss, audience?'

5 *Safety should never be forgotten.* No activity should involve running in a confined space. If youngsters become over-excited, be prepared to sit them down. Never continue with a role play that is drifting away from you

These rules will ensure that role play and practical demonstration are effective tools for teaching and learning in your classroom, but it is also necessary to have a clear view of the rationale for the techniques. Exactly what, in subject and personal development terms, are we hoping to achieve by using these techniques in classes containing children with special educational needs?

Role play as an aid to conceptual understanding

'From concrete to conceptual understanding' (Piaget)
'Experience and do rather than transmit' (Bruner)

Both of the quotations above – brought to my attention by the late Rob Phillips – neatly encapsulate the power of role play and practical demonstration as an active learning technique. All pupils in my experience (and particularly those with special needs) find learning easier when it progresses from concrete, familiar experience towards abstract concept. A pupil experiencing the physical discomfort of lying in close confinement with three others on and under a narrow desk will more easily conceptualise the suffering of slaves in the middle passage, than one merely given an illustration of the layout of a slave ship. Progression from the practical discomfort to the illustration, and then perhaps to a written source, provides access to documents that might otherwise have seemed remote and inaccessible.

Role play as a way of addressing the needs of the kinaesthetic learner

Role play and practical demonstration require movement, and harness it productively to learning. Many youngsters seethe when confined to a desk for long periods – particularly the ADHD child – and see the chance to take part in an active demonstration as a form of liberation. Adherence to the rules outlined earlier will ensure that liberation will not become revolution!

Role play in the quest for empathy

The historical experience is also the human experience. History is of course enquiry, but it is primarily an enquiry into human activity. Pupils have a common humanity with people of the past and therefore the quest to identify with the experiences of those people should not prove over-ambitious. Teenagers find the human experience and human reaction to the continuities and changes of the past a particularly fascinating area of historical study: perhaps because of the process of continuity and change taking place within their own adolescent bodies. Role play exploits this natural affinity and can provide real insight into the ideas and attitudes of the past. Once a pupil of mine, after having taken part in the Reichstag role play, approached me and spontaneously said 'I haven't just learned about the Reichstag – I've *been* in the Reichstag'. That, to me, proved the power of these techniques in addressing KSU 2a of history in the National Curriculum: 'experiences a range of ideas, beliefs and attitudes of men, women and children in the past.'

Causation

Practical demonstration can graphically and memorably illustrate causation. For example, the principal reason for the huge casualties on the Somme becomes plain when the five rounds per second rate of fire of a machine gun is tapped out with echoing resonance on a desk using a plastic board pen, and compared to the relatively snail-like click click . . . bang rate of fire of the bolt action rifle. KSU 2c: 'to analyse and explain the reasons for and results of the historical events, situations and changes in the periods studied' suddenly becomes within reach for all children.

Non-written communication and the writing hook

As a child, I was notoriously ham-fisted in the technology lessons then known as woodwork. After two years of labour I emerged with nothing more than a single $93°$ book end. Fortunately, woodwork and its associated sense of failure only came around once a week. Had I struggled with writing, I would have enjoyed no such interval between failure sessions – I would have had up to six a day. Many children with special needs suffer under such a burden and receive blows to confidence and self-esteem on an hourly basis. Role play can provide a chance to explore ideas without writing. It can also give the opportunity to consolidate ideas in a motivational way as a precursor to a written task. It can provide a writing hook – the impetus to try.

Fun

Never forget that we are teaching children and young people. The young, in particular, respond to fun, yet it is very easy – in the face of mark schemes, subject frameworks, teaching objectives, content overload and Ofsted inspectors – to make the classroom a grey and deadly serious place. Role play and practical demonstration can provide fun with no loss of rigour – and lessons will be the richer for it.

The sample activities are intended as a taster of what is possible. For more ideas see my three articles in *Teaching History* magazine (August 2000, December 2002, December 2003). There are also other ideas on the Historical Association website www.history.org.uk.

My advice is to start simply with the less elaborate demonstrations and role plays. Then, once possibilities are realised, begin to develop ideas of your own!

INSET Activity

Look through the department's schemes of work paying particular attention to the 'Learning Intentions' 'Enquiry Questions' and 'Learning Activities columns'. Can you see a topic where the learning intentions centre on complex causation, difficult concepts or challenging information to recall and use? In other words, the kind of topic teachers approach with a sinking feeling, knowing that a class can easily be switched off by the very detail that seems essential for understanding.

Work in pairs seeking to develop any one of these three types of practical demonstration and role play, working on making existing learning intentions and outcomes more achievable and more enjoyable to achieve:

- *A simple play centred around a significant achievement or act of a controversial figure, such as Cromwell's selection and training of his Ironsides; Mary, Queen of Scots' involvement with Babington, and many more . . .*

- *A quick and practical demonstration to reinforce a concept, such as a lobbed ball of paper to show the trajectory of a nuclear missile, a piece of paper torn up to show the creation of the Polish corridor, and so on . . .*

- *A simple re-enactment allowing pupils to react in role, such as Lenin's speeches promising peace, bread and land to an audience clutching cards outlining social circumstance – wounded soldier, factory owner, widow, peasant, etc.*

You will surprise yourselves!

Three suggested activities involving practical demonstration and role play follow.

Activity 1: practical demonstration to reinforce a concept: the atomic egg

Study unit: A World Study after 1900 at KS3 or any Modern World specification at GCSE

> KSU 2c *'to analyse and explain the reasons for and results of the historical events, situations and changes in the periods studied.'*

The conceptualisation of the relative power of an atomic or hydrogen weapon compared to that of ordinary explosive is often taken for granted by teachers when dealing with topics such as the Hiroshima bomb or the Cuban missile crisis. Children certainly understand that the bang is bigger – but how much bigger? How much more destructive? Video footage does not really bring across any sense of scale. Without the concept of relative power of destruction, understanding of terms such as 'the nuclear threat', 'nuclear balance' or 'mutually assured destruction' must be shaky indeed. Here practical demonstration comes into its own. The expenditure of very little time can bring the concept sought for into stark relief.

Method

1   Take a sheet of A1 sugar paper and mark on it an oval of approximately 30 cm diameter. Write in the oval 'Greater London' and then show pupils a map of the UK with Greater London clearly indicated. This will give an idea of the size of the city compared to the country as a whole.

2   Use a program such as get-a-map (www.ordnancesurvey.org.uk to print out two maps: one of street scale and one of borough scale. These can be compared to the UK map.

3   On the street-scale map explain that one large conventional WW2 bomb would wipe out a block of houses. Mark this on the street map in highlighter pen. Then invite pupils to shade the same explosion on the borough map, then the sugar paper map of London. On this last map, the WW2 bomb would be no larger than the tip of a ballpoint pen.

4   Now take an egg. Explain to pupils that the mess made by this egg will represent the area affected by an atomic explosion. Invite pupils to stand back, then drop the egg from a height of approximately 0.5 metre on the sugar paper oval of 'London'. It will cover the whole area.

5   Now compare that effect to the ballpoint pen dot! The concept of relative destructive power is established.

Follow Up

After this lesson, written and photographic accounts of atomic attack can be studied from a firm conceptual base. Of particular use is the interview with Colonel Tibbets (first pilot to drop an atomic weapon) on the TV series *The World at War* episode, *The Bomb*.

Activity 2: an exercise in contextualisation and analysis of contemporary attitudes: the Trial of Charles I

Study unit: Britain 1500–1750

KSU 2a: *'experiences a range of ideas, beliefs and attitudes of men, women and children in the past.'*

The trial of Charles was a pivotal and unique event in the development of the constitution of England and the relative power of Parliament and the Crown. This role play focuses on the attitude of Parliament's officers towards Charles and vice versa. It avoids complex script by using the thrust of the speeches rather than the actual words used. This allows youngsters to analyse attitude, without the initial detraction of complex language. If desired, the actual language can be approached in a follow-up after the role play, once youngsters' interest and confidence has been established.

The purpose of this role play is to underline the highly controversial nature of the trial and execution of the King. It will highlight:

- the absence of defence counsel

- the King's view that the court had no authority

- the denial, to Charles, of the right to speak

- the charges against Charles

Method

1   You will need four leading pupil volunteers: Charles, Bradshaw and two lawyers. Two fairly restrained 'heavies' to act as soldiers can be useful additions.

2   Brief Charles to sneer at the court and to treat them with contemptuous disdain throughout.

3   Issue speech cards to the principal characters. Inform the rest of the class that they have been specially selected to be hostile to Charles. They must hiss when he enters and mutter approval when he is hustled out. This keeps them involved.

4   Bradshaw enters first, then Charles with his armed escort and, finally, the lawyers for the prosecution. You act as a master of ceremonies, giving pupils the cue to speak etc.

5   The speech cards contain speaking order and, largely, the play runs itself.

6   On the play finishing, give key discussion points to the pupils for paired discussion: Why did Charles treat the court with contempt? Why wouldn't Bradshaw allow the King to speak? Why was there no defence counsel?

Speech Cards for Charles I trial

Bradshaw
(speaks first)

'You, Charles Stuart are charged with

- Taking away the freedom of the people
  - Taking away Parliament's powers
- Making war against your own people.

Lawyers! Press the charges!'

Lawyer One
(speaks second)

'What do you say about all the deaths you have caused? Plead!'

'What do you say about trying to arrest MPs? Plead!'

'What do you say about starting a second war from prison? Plead!'

Lawyer Two
(speaks third)

'What do you say about plotting with foreigners against England? Plead!'

'You are a man of blood. Admit it. Plead!'

'Why are you speechless? ANSWER!!!'

Charles I
(*Speaks after both lawyers have finished*)

'I wish to know by what right I am brought here: by what legal right. Parliament is not a court of law. I will not plead "guilty" or "not guilty" as you are not a judge and this is not a proper court.'

Bradshaw
(speaks fifth)

'Take him away!' . . . . (wait for Charles to go)

'You, Charles Stuart are found guilty of

- Being a murderer
- Being a public enemy
- Being a tyrant'

Activity 3: an exercise in access to and recall of complex causation: Hitler's seizure of power 1932–3

Study Unit: A World study after 1900; GCSE Depth Study or Modern World 'Governments in Action'

> KSU 2c: *'to analyse and explain the reasons for and results of the historical events, situations and changes in the periods studied.'*

Extremely complex topics such as this can lose pupils in a maze of technical terms and complex chronological unfolding of events. While detail is required eventually for full understanding of causation, if tackled too soon it will quickly lead to 'switch off' for most of the class. It is hard to rescue a child's confidence after pessimism about 'getting it' has set in, yet it is eminently possible to raise the level of detail and analysis once broad understanding and, therefore, confidence has been established. A simplified role play can illustrate the framework of the topic in an enjoyable way, grab enthusiasm, and pave the way for methodical analysis of the political moves of 1932–33.

Method

1   Arrange the class in three blocks with the largest formed of the quietest pupils in the centre. The left-hand block of about six represent Communists. The right-hand block represents Nazis. This block should be larger.

2   Take Nazis and Communists out of the room to brief them. Leave classroom door open or observe through glass door the antics of those still in the room, but remember that these were selected as the quietest.

3   Communists are briefed to shout down with Nazis whenever Nazis make a noise. They are told to stop as Nazis stop.

4   Nazis are told to look to their leader. A charismatic pupil is essential for this. He or she is told to give a signal to the Nazis to shout and yell as any democratic politician speaks. Nazis are briefed to be absolutely silent on a signal from their leader.

5   From the centre, select two chancellors – one to succeed the other. Give them a pre-written speech of dull content. Three lines will suffice as Nazi interruptions will prevent the speech from being heard. Centre is briefed to give polite applause on a new chancellor standing.

6   The teacher, as Von Hindenburg, the German President, makes a play of having to choose a chancellor in this time of crisis. He pointedly shows contempt for the Communists, and expresses fear that they will confiscate his own wealth and land pours scorn on the Nazi leader as an ex-corporal and selects a chancellor from the centre.

7   On starting his/her acceptance speech, the new Chancellor is howled down by the Nazis and the din is joined by Communist shouts. The Chancellor is

dismissed by the teacher as incompetent and the noise stops on a signal from the Nazis' leader.

8   This is repeated with the same result. The teacher then selects the Nazi leader and makes him Chancellor. The centre politely applauds. Communists remain silent from fear of the larger Nazi block.

9   Subsequent events such as the elimination of the Communists and the intimidation of the centre can be explained and, after acting a dramatic yet natural death for Hindenburg, the teacher can easily ask the class where power in Germany now lies.

This role play is noisy, but its power is unmatched for showing how a rule-respecting centre can be undermined by a combination of organised disruption and prejudice from those entrusted with guarding the constitution. Detailed follow-up is easy, and to any depth required. Pupils will have gained interest and, just as important, confidence that the topic is indeed understandable.

(This is an extract from my article in *Teaching History*, August 2000.)

Case Study – Sarah, a pupil with Asperger's Syndrome

Sarah finds it difficult to remember large amounts of information at the same time – particularly if given in extended verbal form. She also finds it difficult to remember instructions unless these are given in manageable chunks with a pause for assimilation between each discrete step. Long text extracts (whether read aloud by pupil or teacher) will challenge her to the point where frustration may lead to anger expressed through verbal outbursts or shrieks. Behaviour can be challenging at times since Sarah will fidget and occasionally call out if frustrated. She has been known to leave her seat and wander about during periods of extended teacher talk.

Sarah's popularity within the class is low. Her desperate desire for friends and her inability to read non-verbal signals from her peers tends to lead her to invade personal space or to make inappropriate or ill-timed comments. She finds it particularly difficult to cope with groups of other children and will occasionally become over-stimulated to the point that she swears or even, rarely, spits.

Sarah will often repeat complex language and recycle it – apparently in context – leading teachers unfamiliar with her to believe that she has an impressive grasp of a topic or skill. In reality, she often does not understand the meaning of the words she is using. This said, her ability to understand complex ideas is not markedly different from other pupils of her age as long as she is not presented with too many at once. Sarah's speech patterns do not immediately make her noticeable, although occasionally she does lapse into a monotone.

Calmness of approach and calmness of voice work well with Sarah. She also responds well to established routine and can react adversely when this is changed without warning. If unsettled, she can challenge the teacher quite considerably, with a tendency to repeat questions, words and phrases. In such a situation, repetition of answer or instruction from the teacher is to be avoided as the start of a spiral towards over-stimulus. Gentle diversion of attention can work well in this situation. Sarah does not like to sit still for long periods. A five-minute 'walk around' is very effective at calming Sarah down.

Strengths:

Sarah's reading age is on a par with her chronological age and she reads short extracts aloud quite effectively. Her drawing ability is outstanding, particularly when the subject matter is roof lines, human hairstyles or hats! She is gifted in mathematics, particularly in topics dealing with shape or space. Her capacity for mental computation of number can be breathtaking.

General IEP targets:

- to avoid calling out in class (Sarah has been encouraged to write questions down when she cannot get the teacher's attention);
- to work co-operatively with other pupils in group work situations;
- to ask for help if unsure of instructions.

Lesson background:

This mixed ability Year 8 class had studied the build up to the English Civil War, using study of a sequence of Parliament's demands and Charles I's responses to illustrate the different perspectives and widening gulf between the positions and attitudes of the two sides. They had then gone on to study the war itself with the objective of understanding the bitter and bloody nature of the conflict. Involvement in the heart of the battle re-enactment role play used as part of this study could have been a source of over-stimulus for Sarah. This was avoided by her inclusion as the general giving commands. The class now had a context for study of the trial of Charles I.

Lesson objectives:

The pupils will be able to:

- understand why Charles I's trial was unique;
- appreciate the attitudes and beliefs of defendant and prosecutors;
- make basic comparisons between Charles' trial and a modern trial;
- use knowledge of the context of the trial as a basis for subsequent, more detailed exploration of the enquiry question 'Was Charles I treated fairly?'

Sarah's objectives for this lesson:

I see no reason why Sarah should be given different objectives to those of the rest of the class. The use of role play rather than traditional analysis of accounts of the trial should be an answer to her difficulty in processing too much verbal information at one time. Participation as one of the lawyers will allow her to move around and will make use of her ability to read aloud.

Activities:

1. Pupils were asked to think back to the last TV trial they had seen. Examples could be of the type of the 'Who shot Phil?' trial from *Eastenders* or, more recently, the trial of Rita from *Coronation Street*. A clip of such a trial could be shown. Pupils were given cards marked: 'The person accused of a crime'; 'The lawyer trying to prove the accused person is not guilty'; 'The lawyer trying to prove the accused person is guilty'; 'The person making sure that both lawyers have a fair chance to put their case'; 'The right of all to be heard'. Link the character cards with the characters shown in the clip if a video extract is to be used.

2. Pupils were then asked to take away any one of the cards *except* the 'person accused of a crime' card. They were then asked as a class what the effect on the trial would be. Answers edged towards the idea of unfairness and pupils were then pushed to say *why* removal of one element would make a trial unfair. Sarah was well capable of following such short directed tasks. Calling out was discouraged by referring to it as unfair. A TA sat with Sarah, indicating a good time to raise a hand if necessary.

3. The class then went into the role play 'The Trial of Charles I'. 'Bradshaw' was equipped with a steel helmet from the department museum. Sarah was given the part of the second lawyer – she had enjoyed speaking aloud in the battle reconstruction role play and readily accepted the part. As

second lawyer she had a clear cue when to speak – as soon as the first lawyer had finished – and, therefore, was not expected to take a cue from another pupil's gesture or expression. The part is short and dramatic, ending with a purposeful shout. If another pupil had been keen on the lawyer role, the whole role play is short enough to run through again with a different part allocation – Sarah would then be involved as one of the audience in Westminster Hall, hissing at the right times with the others!

4. Pupils were then asked to list as many reasons as they could why the trial of Charles seemed unfair. Which elements of the previously discussed trial were missing? These reasons were then shared in discussion. Sarah had the ability to take full part in the discussion – an ability reinforced by the chance to prepare in a brief written task.

5. Analysis then took place of Charles' final (interrupted) speech, of the lawyers' accusations, and of Bradshaw's summing up – each child was given a written copy of these. The class were asked to underline Charles' reasons for treating the court so disrespectfully, then the court's reasons for seeing Charles as no ordinary criminal.

6. The next lesson would see the use of a writing frame as scaffold to help the class answer the enquiry question 'Was Charles I's trial fair?' Further differentiated research through the use of ICT would build on the enthusiasm and accessibility engendered by the role play.

Points to note about the lesson:

Sarah should have benefited from the lesson in a number of ways. She was given card stimulus to help her recall key elements of trials and then to contribute without frustration to the discussion on 'fairness'. Interruption was associated with unfairness in her mind – a message to be built upon in subsequent lessons. Sarah's part in the role play helped her relate to previous contributions by others – she needed to use timing, yet her cue was clear and did not present an insurmountable challenge. Her self-esteem would have been enhanced by the use of her strength at reading aloud, and she was allowed to leave her seat for a purpose (perhaps noting a different reaction from inappropriate desertion of her seat in other lessons), and making fidgeting less likely in the later part of the lesson. Even a shout in role was permitted: gently reinforcing the idea of appropriate time for certain actions. Finally, a complex topic was addressed without long periods of verbal input from the teacher.

Case study – Harry, a pupil with dyslexia

Harry is a friendly, outgoing boy. He enjoys learning but is increasingly frustrated as he grows older with the subjects associated with significant amounts of written work – most of them, it seems to him! For Harry, PE, drama and technology lessons are a breath of fresh air. He finds science practicals fun, but the writing up of the experiments frequently leaves the pleasure of the practical achievement a distant memory.

Harry enjoys the subject matter of history – he has built his own model of the Western Front in enormous detail and is hooked on the History Channel, but in Year 9, as options loom, he feels it would be far more sensible to drop the subject. Geography, with its maps and diagrams, seems tempting: so much of historical study seems to depend on reading and writing.

Harry can read but he finds it exhausting and laborious, even with his tinted glasses. Writing is torture for him as his dyslexia is so severe that teachers find his work completely misrepresentative of his true level of understanding. Yet a piece of written work that takes others ten minutes to complete can take Harry an hour – all for teachers to ask him to explain it to them orally. Harry can use a laptop to improve presentation, but the spell checker cannot recognise Harry's version of words, so it tends to increase his frustration at times. Harry is embarrassed working one-to-one with a TA.

Harry is spectacularly successful in debate and his oral answers display a sophisticated understanding of the whole range of the Knowledge, Skills and Understanding of the National Curriculum – providing long, complex sources are read to him and he is allowed to express his ideas orally. At KS3 this form of assessment is not precluded yet, to Harry, it seems all-too-rare.

Strengths:
Harry is lucid and has a high level of verbal reasoning skill. He is highly intelligent and perceptive and displays strong self-confidence – until a book, written source or pen is placed in front of him. He excels at mathematics.

Harry is popular with teachers and pupils alike. He tries hard and generally behaves well (although he would admit to a drifting of attention during written tasks). He is particularly good at penetrating to the heart of a topic with precise questioning.

General IEP targets:
- to continue attending spelling club;
- to use his laptop for written tasks.

Lesson background:
The class had just finished studying the causes of the Great Depression of the 1930s. They had looked at the particular difficulties affecting Germany in the early 1920s and in the early 1930s. They had dealt with the ideas of the Nazi party and had examined the motivation of many of its supporters. Their understanding of Communism arose from study of the Russian Revolution earlier in the term.

Lesson objectives:

The pupils will be able to:

- explain how Nazi tactics succeeded in giving them power;
- understand the attitudes of President Hindenburg towards political extremists;
- form hypotheses of developments after January 1933;
- address the enquiry question 'Why did Hitler come to power in 1933?'

Harry's objectives for this lesson:

Harry's objectives will be identical to those of all the other pupils. He will be encouraged to fill in 'thought bubbles' for Hitler and Hindenburg using his laptop and the 'call out' template in Microsoft Word, but will be allowed to express his ideas for the enquiry question orally on tape for homework.

Activities:

1. The class examined Reichstag election results for July 1932 on a semi-circular diagram showing the number of seats held by all parties. By simple arithmetic they worked out the number of seats required for an overall majority and how far short the Nazis were of that number.

2. The class then looked at photographs of the massed ranks of Hitler's SA. The scene of the SA beating up the nightclub owner from *Cabaret* is particularly effective at underlining the nature of the organisation. They were asked, 'How could these men be used by Hitler to apply pressure to those in power in Germany in 1932?'

3. The 'Hitler's Seizure of Power' role play was then used. Harry was given the role of Hitler or the Communist leader, Thalmann. These parts both demand charisma but involve no writing or reading.

4. At the end of the role play debrief, pupils in role asked questions like, 'Why did Hindenburg not choose a Communist leader?' 'How did Hitler ensure that the democratic leaders were ineffective?'

5. This was then followed by placing large cardboard 'thought bubbles' above the head of the character who played Hitler and above each pupil's own head as Hindenburg. Pupils were invited to write thoughts in their own copies of the bubbles as to each character's hopes and intentions in the years to come. Harry used his laptop for this.

6. In the next lesson, sources were used to deepen understanding. Harry, as one of the key participants of the role play, now had the incentive to tackle sources that might have seemed impossible to him before the role play. He did accept help from the TA and, with her, planned his response to the enquiry question. He recorded an in-depth answer on tape and gained a level 7 for his efforts.

Points to note about the lesson:

Harry's participation as one of the key figures of the role play enthused him to the extent that he was able to tackle written sources and accept help in doing so. It also made use of his strengths of charisma and popularity. The role play gave access to the causation of a highly complex topic and gave Harry and other pupils the confidence to form hypotheses. Allowing Harry to tackle the enquiry question on tape saved him the frustration of being unable to release his ideas onto paper, yet the thought bubble exercise gave him a written task to practise his skills upon.

CHAPTER 7

Monitoring and Assessment

Assessment

Assessment provides feedback on the progress pupils make, but more importantly it needs to be used to indicate what areas need to be improved and how that can be achieved. An issue for teachers is how to communicate judgements about achievement and effort to pupils in an accessible way.

Too often assessment can be a closed book to pupils, known only by teachers, and communicated by either a grade or a mark to a pupil. Do pupils know what 7/10 or a level 4 means? Do they know why they got that mark rather than 8/10 or a level 5? Do they know what they can do to improve next time they are assessed?

If pupils are to understand and benefit from being assessed they need to be taught how to carry out assessment themselves. This works at several levels: they need to share or participate in setting the assessment objectives; they need to be involved in the assessing of work either through self or peer assessment; and they need to consider how to use the information to improve their work in future.

The KS3 Strategy in the Foundation subjects offers some interesting thoughts here. In terms of formative assessment, the following process is suggested:

- The teacher explains what the pupils need to include in their work.

- The pupils then do the work.

- They discuss in groups whether they have met these criteria.

- They share their ideas with the class, who in turn comment on how well the criteria have been met.

- The rest of the class then offer suggestions about what the group could do to improve the work.

In terms of group work situations this has great potential, but it can also apply to any other piece of work. For example, with written work, pupils could be paired up as assessment partners, whose job it is to offer critical feedback on each other's piece of work. The aim is to help them both improve their grades, by enabling them to help each other. To do this, the class needs to be clear about the particular features the teacher is looking for within a piece of work. It may be something as simple as writing in paragraphs, with each paragraph being about a distinct idea, or something more sophisticated about the value of sources (see below for a further discussion of a possible approach with this).

The following example comes from an exercise with my bottom set Year 11 group. They were doing the history of medicine and I was trying to prepare them for tackling the source-based paper. As a class we went through the sources, summarising each in three to five words, so they could navigate their way round them quickly later. They were then presented with the mark scheme for this particular paper. In small groups of two or three they then had to produce on OHT an answer to a given question, which the rest of the class would comment on, using the mark scheme to give a mark and reasons for the mark awarded.

One group had to compare two sources about the Plague of 1665 in London. The sources are given below:

Source 3 – Orders by the Lord Mayor of London in 1665

'Women searchers in every parish to report whether the person do die of the Infection.

As soon as any man shall be found to be sick of the plague, he shall be shut up in his house. The house shall be shut up for a month.

The constable to see every shut up house be attended with watchmen. The watchmen shall get food for the people. This shall be paid for at public expense if they cannot afford it themselves.'

> **Source 4 – From *The Plague and the Fire*, a book written by the historian James Leasor in 1962**
>
> 'London depended on the farms around its wall for milk and food. Only the Lord Mayor's intelligent action saved the city from famine. Sir John Lawrence ordered his city officers to organise special routes for the country people who brought food in to the markets. They would not see and be frightened by the sights so familiar to Londoners: piles of bodies naked and dead on the stinking carts; mounds of corpses waiting on the edge of mass burial grounds.'

The question for the group was 'compare the value of these sources for a historian enquiring into the role of the Lord Mayor during the Plague.'

The mark scheme was as follows:

Level 1 – Simple undeveloped statement(s) offering valid point(s) 1–2

Level 2 – Developed statement based on content of source with some reference to nature/origin

e.g. describes actions taken to stop the spread of plague and keep supplies moving

Or expands on value of source in the light of nature/origin of source and makes some reference to content 3–5

Level 3 – Reasoned discussion of value. Considers contribution of source content in the light of the nature and/or origin of the sources

e.g. explores the value and implications of the orders issued and compares the value of the historians' overview and judgement. Shows Leasor puts the role of the mayor in context. 6–8

Mark schemes contain complicated language for less able children as a lot of it is 'history teacher speak', so as a class we focus on the distinction between a simple statement and a developed statement, as these phrases regularly occur and are the difference between a level 1 and 2 answer. Pupils were also reminded of what is meant by nature/origin of the source.

The pupils' initial answer was:

We can see that source 3 was orders by the Lord Mayor to help prevent the spread of the plague. Source 4 tells us about what actually happens about the plague. From source 3 we can see that people were shut up in their houses and a watchman was guarding their houses to stop them running away and spreading the infection to nearby towns.

The discussion about this answer showed that pupils felt it was easily a level 1 answer. Pupils liked the last sentence, as it seemed to develop the reason for having watchmen. But they were not sure whether it hit the criteria for level 2, which requires some reference to the nature/origin of the sources. They felt the first sentence hinted at this but was not clear enough. In response, the group took their answer and added another sentence onto the end:

Source 3 shows us that their are orders given by the Lord Mayor but source 4 is more valuable in that it shows us what happened by the people of the towns.

Clearly, there was more that needed to be dealt with, even with the addition of this sentence, but the sentence did add to the answer, was in response to comments from the rest of the class, and showed that the pupils were trying to get to grips with how they could actually improve their answers.

Once pupils become more skilled in understanding what the teacher is looking for within a piece of work, then they could be asked themselves what might make a good answer. I much prefer to ask what would make a better 'history' answer, than how this level 3 answer could be made into a level 4. Partly this is due to the way that levels have become misused within assessment, but it also gets away from the obsession with providing levels – let us focus on the subject and what makes for a good answer within the demands of the subject.

If pupils are involved in this process of helping to assess work, they will get to understand the process better by taking ownership of it, rather than trying to interpret the teacher's judgement.

Assessment objectives

If pupils do not understand what they are being assessed against, then it is not surprising if they fail to produce good pieces of work in response to a question. Look at the following questions:

1   What were conditions on slave ships during the Middle Passage really like?

2   How can we find out about conditions on slave ships during the Middle Passage?

3   Why do historians disagree over the abolition of slavery?

4   Why was slavery abolished?

5   How could slave traders justify their trade?

6   Why was the slave trade important?

7   Why is the slave trade important?

Each question is different, some subtly so, but would pupils be aware of the differences? Questions 1, 3 and 7 address the issue of interpretation, question 2 is more directly concerned with working with sources, questions 4 and 6 are primarily concerned with causal reasoning, while question 5 is trying to elicit some form of empathetic understanding. We need to be careful in our phrasing of questions and what sort of response they require.

At an Ofsted conference on assessment, one school had carefully mapped out their assessment questions across the key stage. It included two similar questions: 'Was William the Conqueror a good king?' and 'Was King John a bad king?' yet each question was testing a completely different key element – the first was focused on working with sources, while the second was looking at interpretations. Obviously, the focus of each question was discussed with the pupils, but the opportunity for confusion exists. Questions that are more carefully phrased, e.g. 'Do the sources suggest William the Conqueror was a good king?' and 'Why are there such different views about whether King John was a bad king?' address the key elements more explicitly. Obviously, there may be a need to introduce greater complexity into questions that require handling of sources, interpretations and so on, but it makes sense, in the first place, to use clear questions, and then develop the level of complexity as part of progression across Key Stages 3 and 4. Part of progression is the setting of more complex questions where pupils will need to use several skills together to reach an answer.

Consider, for example, the idea of causation. What questions might be asked that demonstrate greater levels of complexity and therefore progression?

- Describe what events led to William's victory at Hastings in 1066.

- Why did William win the Battle of Hastings?

- What was the most important reason why William won the Battle of Hastings?

- To what extent was William's victory at Hastings down to good fortune?

Each question is essentially based around causation, but look at it in slightly different ways, that offer potentially greater challenge. It is clear that a question like 'why did x happen' could equally well be asked of a five-year-old, a GCSE student and an undergraduate, who would all be able to create valid responses, but those responses would be hugely different.

However, the first question would be the most likely to produce a narrative of events. The second question could be answered in a number of different ways, depending on how the pupils are taught to think about it. The pupils might have looked at the battle chronologically, and would therefore produce a narrative of events, with some commentary on different factors that led to the Norman victory. However, if the pupils had been taught to categorise the factors under certain headings then this should come through in the writing. Alternatively, pupils may well have been asked to think about causes in order of importance. So, even within a question, the range of responses could be different. The important distinction here is how the pupils are taught to think about the problem of causation, as this will influence how they organise their writing. The third question is far more firmly focused on the issue of importance. This can prove difficult for pupils, as there is technically no right answer, so the quality of the response is dependent on the reasoning behind their choice of factor. The final question requires a greater degree of judgement.

Asking the right question, both in terms of focus and level of difficulty is clearly vital. Having a clear question, though, is not the end of the story. Pupils need to discuss the question in order to deepen their understanding of what needs to be addressed. At the start of a lesson this may involve reference back to the previous lesson, or even reference to work centred on a similar style of question. When looking at the origins of the First World War, pupils may recall work carried out on the origins of the English Civil War, with useful comparisons being made as a starting point – e.g. pupils might be asked to recall the reasons for the Civil War but then asked to hypothesise as to whether these reasons would still be valid in the context of the early twentieth century. Similarly, when analysing the impact of the ideas of Charles Darwin, pupils might recall and compare the impact that the ideas of the Scientific Revolution had on people. Not only will this generate preliminary discussion, but it also starts to produce an insight into the purpose of the likely assessment.

Figure 7.1 looks at some possible questions that might be asked when examining whether the Great Reform Act of 1832 was truly great. The questions vary from knowledge of the workings of Parliament, links to similar work, broader contextual questions and questions about the actual Reform Act itself. All may need to be asked to help pupils understand the big question. Part of the trick of successful teaching is knowing which questions to ask and when.

Questions about working of Parliament	Questions about earlier work	Questions providing further context about period	Questions judging impact of Reform Act
What was Parliament? How was it organised?	Where have you heard about Parliament before?	How had the way people lived changed in that time?	What did the 1832 Reform Act change?
What role did it play in running the country?	How important was Parliament in these earlier times?	Why was there pressure to change the franchise? Or why did more people want to vote?	Did more people get the vote? How happy would people have been with the changes to who could vote?
What was wrong with Parliament during the early part of the nineteenth century?	How had Parliament's power changed since earlier times?		
What could be done to improve the way Parliament governed?			

Figure 7.1 *Asking the right questions*

Pupils also need help in selecting appropriate information for an answer. Near the end of a topic, pupils need to consider what they have studied and what is directly relevant to the question being asked. A question such as 'Why did Britain become a Protestant nation during the sixteenth century? With what consequences did Britain become a Protestant nation?' covers a great deal of taught material differences between Catholic and Protestant churches:

- Henry VIII's divorce and subsequent break with Rome

- Henry VIII and his six wives

- the Dissolution of the Monasteries

- the religious swings under Edward VI, Mary and Elizabeth

- the reputation of Mary

- the problems facing Elizabeth

- the growing antipathy towards Catholics caused by the Gunpowder Plot

Having taught all of this, with the main question kept firmly in place during the sequence of lessons, pupils then have to create a menu of material they have been taught, decide which material is directly relevant to the question, and decide which material will answer the question regarding 'why' and which will address the issue of 'with what consequences'. To make this more active and allow the pupils to experiment with ideas, the pupils could arrange cards or post-it notes under appropriate headings. This could be done on large pieces of card, a flip chart or whiteboard. This has the benefit of allowing the pupils to try out their ideas without penalty, as mistakes can be easily rectified. This level of discussion will clarify the assessment objectives or will identify where pupils need further direction. Hopefully, by the time the question is tackled, this should not be an issue, as one of the uses of formative assessment in history is to monitor what pupils have understood as the teaching unfolds. In other words, do pupils know the different reasons for Henry VIII's divorce, and can they explain the problems Elizabeth I encountered at the start of her reign and how far she had tackled them by the end, before they actually get to the final piece of work?

Another way of helping pupils understand further the importance of the selection and handling of material is to provide two slightly different questions. As well as asking, 'Why did Britain become a Protestant nation?' the pupils could be asked, 'Explain which was the most important reason for Britain becoming a Protestant nation.'

Assessing work

At a more detailed level, pupils need to be aware of what constitutes appropriate answers and why some answers are better than others. To be able to do this, they need a clear understanding of the constituent parts required within an answer.

If we consider a question such as 'Using the sources, explain what you think conditions in nineteenth-century factories were like', we need to think about what skills such a question is assessing. It is obviously linked to working with sources, but which source skills in particular might be expected? There is an obvious need for comprehension, but the question also probably requires comparison, explanation for different viewpoints, resolution of conflict between sources, and criteria to reach a reasoned judgement. It is also a written assignment that requires structure and logical construction, as well as clarity in description. A simple ticklist might help pupils make sense of what they need to put in the answer:

- Are all the sources referred to?

- Does the answer show what the sources agree on?

- Does the answer show what the sources disagree on?

- Does the answer explain why the sources disagree?

- Does the answer say which sources are the best to use, and why?

- Is it well written?

Pupils, therefore, need to be aware of these, but also to comprehend what they look like. This is where the importance of modelling can come in – the teacher can model what a good explanation would look like:

Both sources A and C show that conditions in the factories were harsh. They both mention long working hours, over 14 hours a day. Source A mentions that children were so tired that they often fell asleep. C mentions there were many accidents. What is described in source C might explain the accidents in A. B, however, disagrees, and says that the children were well looked after, had the chance to earn good money, and could get some schooling at certain points in the day.

Such an answer could be discussed, and strengths and weaknesses picked out to help pupils gain a better idea of how to approach the answer.

Alternatively, get the pupils to elaborate on a starter sentence:

- Both sources agree . . .

- Both sources disagree over . . .

- The reason they disagree is . . .

- The best source to use is . . . because . . .

This can then be shared in discussion, and ideas compared. A game could be developed here, for example Hammond's (2002) idea of throwing factual punches to knock out an opponent. In this situation, pupils have to argue from different perspectives, one arguing conditions were dreadful, and the other that conditions were not as bad as they were made out to be. Pupils would have to use information from the sources, but also attack the nature and origin of the sources as a way of undermining their opponents. A pair of opposing pupils step into the imaginary boxing ring and deliver their 'punch' or opening argument – whoever is judged to have the better 'punch', stays in, while another opponent enters the ring, and so it continues. This would demonstrate the value of precise factual knowledge and analysis of the sources. In turn, this would show the importance of explanatory sentences.

Another idea is that pupils could play a game where they have to pass an answer backwards and forwards between themselves, adding points to a sentence or paragraph to improve it, until the sentence or paragraph is complete – whoever finishes the section gains the point. A model answer can be analysed and good points within the answer can be highlighted and weaker bits could be modified to show how they could be improved.

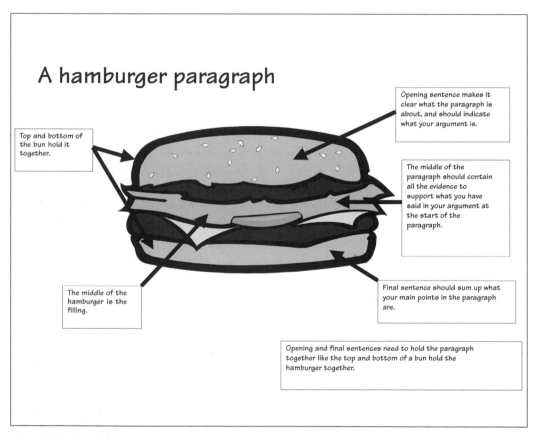

A hamburger paragraph

Top and bottom of the bun hold it together.

Opening sentence makes it clear what the paragraph is about, and should indicate what your argument is.

The middle of the paragraph should contain all the evidence to support what you have said in your argument at the start of the paragraph.

The middle of the hamburger is the filling.

Final sentence should sum up what your main points in the paragraph are.

Opening and final sentences need to hold the paragraph together like the top and bottom of a bun hold the hamburger together.

Figure 7.2 A hamburger paragraph

Often pupils need help at the paragraph level of writing. Many strategies exist to help structure this, such as the use of 'big' points and 'little' points, 'hamburger' paragraphs (see Figure 7.2) or 'evidence sandwiches', as popularised by Mulholland and Banham but Bakalis 2003 stresses even more the need to work through the thinking process when writing a paragraph. Such thinking is difficult for pupils, but to avoid it is not going to help them – they need to be aware of how they can think their way through a process if they are to stand any chance of mastering it. By focusing on the paragraph, Bakalis 2003: 20 states:

. . . it should help pupils to track and view their thinking as it unfolds. Given that memory and concentration are the fundamental problems with lower attainers, the paragraph is a useful, manageable chunk of extended thinking where pupils can see what it is that they have thought without their memories collapsing under the load.

Pupils may be able to link coherent points together, but not necessarily unpack their thinking further. If we take an everyday example that I often use, pupils have to explain why they came to school that day. Responses may include, 'Because my alarm clock went off'; 'My mum kicked me out of the house'; 'I wanted to see my friends'; 'I have to' (note they don't usually refer to getting an education or because they like it!), but they then need to be pressed to take their explanation further. Challenge them with 'Why?' or get them to use a connective to link their initial statement and their explanation. Then bring in a history example:

Q 'Why was Charles Darwin such a dangerous man?

A Because he had new ideas.

Q Why are new ideas 'dangerous'?

A Because they are different.

Q (extend thinking) What was different about these ideas?

A He came up with the theory of evolution.

Q (push it a bit further) What made this such a new idea?

A It challenged the way that people thought about how life was formed, it challenged the accepted view that God had made the world in seven days . . .'

Once these ideas become more concrete through talk and modelling, then they can be transferred to the construction of written paragraphs or talking paragraphs.

To enhance the value of assessment at this stage, pupils also need to be involved in marking either their own work or the work of their peers. Again, for this to be successful, pupils need to be clear about what exactly is being assessed and what this looks like in reality. Given these criteria, pupils can then give themselves a grade, level or comment. This can be achieved easily by presenting pupils with marking criteria on an A4 sheet given to them (either as a tick box approach or level of response mark scheme) with the task. The task should include a section for their own mark and comment (see Figure 7.3 for an example – it is worth thinking deeply about which approach you feel would be more helpful to the pupil)

When being marked by the teacher, one of the things to consider is the extent to which pupils are successful in evaluating their own performance. Not only does this give an insight into the pupil's performance but also into how well they are able to perceive their own performance. This is a crucial area to develop

Tick list approach

Does the answer give several different reasons?
Have the reasons been grouped into paragraphs?
Have connectives been used to explain why so much damage was caused?
Have connectives been used to link different reasons together?
Is it clear which reasons are more important?
Does the answer have an introduction and conclusion?

Level of response approach

Level 1 – gives several different reasons, but these are not grouped together or clearly explained.
Level 2 – gives several different reasons, which are grouped together. The answer will be written in paragaphs.
Level 3 – gives several different reasons, which are grouped together. Why each reason caused so much damage is explained, using connectives. The answer will be written in paragraphs.
Level 4 – gives several different reasons, which are grouped together. Why each reason caused so much damage is explained, using connectives. In addition, links between different reasons are clearly made and the particular importance of certain reasons is explained. The answer will be written in paragraphs.

Figure 7.3 *Why did the Great Fire of London cause so much damage?*

if pupils are to be helped to make significant progress. Often, although pupils find it difficult to make accurate judgements on their own work initially, they are able to do so when considering the work of others.

It is important if peer marking is to be used that there is an air of mutual trust and respect within the classroom so that it can be carried out sensitively. At first, it would probably be best to start with an assessment partner who would provide initial comments. This could then develop into whole-class discussion, using the comments made to discuss what constitutes a good answer.

Areas for improvement

If pupils are aware of the marking criteria, then it should be clear to them, once they receive feedback on their work, what is required to make further improvement. This does, though, require a good understanding of what constitutes progress in history on the part of the class teacher. The National Curriculum levels provide an outline of what is understood by progression, but this provides a very rough guide to progression and in places does not completely match what happens in practice. Part of level 3 states: 'They (pupils) use sources of information in ways that go beyond simple observations to answer questions about the past.' This idea of making inferences from sources is thus seen as quite a low-level skill, yet it can be something that sixth formers and undergraduates can find taxing, depending on the material that is presented.

The image in Figure 7.4 accompanied a novel about the life of a poor orphan boy in the nineteenth century. The novel, by Frances Trollope, was a sad story about the difficulties the orphan boy encountered. The author was obviously writing with a particular intent.

Figure 7.4

What inferences can be made from this? Pupils might infer that:

1 Working conditions in factories were harsh.

2 Working conditions **seem** harsh.

3 This is part of a campaign to improve conditions so conditions must have been harsh.

4 This is the type of method used in such a campaign.

5 Campaigns of this type were aimed at the middle and upper classes because they were literate and they were seen as the ones with the power to bring about the necessary improvements.

All these inferences are possible, but are different. The first two refer specifically to the content of the source, the third and fourth inferences to the nature of the source, while the fifth draws on wider contextual knowledge. They also seem to me to represent varying degrees of complexity of thought, so to label all of them as level 3 would be unfair. They also indicate the sorts of thinking we need to get pupils engaged in. Pupils need to be taught this explicitly if they are to develop this thinking. Questions that focus purely on identifying the source will elicit responses such as the first two examples. This may well be acceptable for some pupils and constitute an achievement, but they also ought to be exposed to more difficult lines of thought. To get to responses like 3 and 4 they need to be questioned about what type of source is being used, why it was produced and what it tells us about what people thought was important or wanted to achieve. Responses like 5 can only come with secure prior knowledge of other areas of history and skilful questioning that will push pupils into that line of thought: Who was this produced for? What makes you think that? Why produce it for that sort of person? If we are, therefore, thinking about moving pupils on from levels 2 or 3, careful consideration needs to be given to what exactly you as a history teacher are looking for to merit the award of such a level – the clearer you are about this, the more clearly this can be communicated to the pupils, so helping them identify how they can progress.

We therefore have to consider progression in a broader context. Progression in history depends on:

- securing a deeper understanding of historical skills and concepts;

- a broader knowledge to use as a framework of reference;

- the complexity of material being studied.

All of these can be pathways for progression. It is important when planning for progression to deliberately plant prior experiences for pupils to draw upon. The guidance in the QCA Schemes of Work for history 2000 offer sensible questions to consider when planning for progression:

- Which ideas and concepts in history depend on a secure understanding of other ideas and concepts?

- How can units be sequenced so that earlier work lays the foundation for later work?

- When ideas and concepts are revisited or reinforced is it in a different context or using different activities?

If we consider the following question we can start to see what we need to do when planning for such progression:

When was Britain closest to revolution in the period 1815 to 1832?

- *Skills* – This question requires pupils to make a judgement; it needs them to understand the significance of events within the timeframe; it may require the ability to handle source material.

- *Concepts* – Pupils need to understand what is meant by revolution; what causes revolutions; how governments can control a country and the limits of that control.

- *Knowledge* – Pupils need to know about conditions prior to other revolutions or revolts; knowledge of the problems with nineteenth-century Britain.

- *Complexity of material* – This depends on the class and their ability.

The following questions indicate how progression can be planned over time:

- Why was the medieval Church so powerful? (Year 7)

- Why was the Scientific Revolution so significant? (Year 8)

- Why was Charles Darwin seen by many to be a dangerous man? (Year 9)

Each question is aimed at examining the mentality of an era. They examine how religious belief came to be undermined and, essentially, replaced by scientific thought and reasoning. The questions, therefore, build up a contextual framework which enables the pupils to understand each new question. In this way, pupils can see the importance of ideas at a particular point in time and, therefore, see what was new. The questions all ask why, which can be made more complex over time from mono-causal reasoning to multi-causal reasoning, and categorisation or linking of ideas to create a web of reasons (as mentioned previously). The materials used can obviously be made more complex.

For the medieval Church, there are many powerful images showing Heaven and Hell as viewed by people of the time. These can provide an accessible means of grasping what people were fearful of, thus emphasising the power of the Church. Pupils could be expected to provide mono or multi-causal reasons for the power of the Church.

When studying the Scientific Revolution, pupils could do a Hall of Fame style gallery of different characters. Using textbooks and other resources, they could examine the achievements of these people, and explain why they deserve to be granted a place in the gallery. This is more complex than the earlier task on the Church, essentially because of the amount of material that is presented to pupils, but also requires a judgement to be reached as to why certain people deserve to be remembered. The level of reasoning is, therefore, more demanding than the medieval example, but links could be made to this earlier work for pupils to build upon. In addition, it requires pupils to appreciate what life was like before and after the Scientific Revolution to see its impact. This provides progression from the earlier work, because it gets pupils to understand how new ideas attacked and undermined the religious beliefs held in medieval times.

When looking at Darwin, the difficulty would arise from the need to understand the concept of evolution and how it conflicted with belief in divine intention. Contemporary sources would be used, requiring contextual knowledge to make sense of them. The type or amount of material could be adapted to make this task more complex than the previous ones. Only by understanding the strength of long-held beliefs can pupils start to appreciate how radical Darwin's ideas were. This builds on the previous work by looking at religious beliefs and the growth of scientific thinking, which then collided dramatically with Darwin's new ideas. Pupils can, therefore, use their contextual knowledge to help them. Again, pupils need to explain their answers. It is possible to build on their previous attempts to do so, by challenging them to produce higher level answers.

However, it is important to recognise that progression can mean different things for different pupils, as pupils with different needs have different priorities. As a form tutor in the early 1990s, I had a boy with Asperger's Syndrome in my class, who received in-class support from a TA. At the time there was little awareness of the needs of a child with such specific problems. Great consternation was caused one day when he asked the TA whether he could fondle her breasts! The assistant was embarrassed, the head was outraged and the parents were called into school. On hearing what had happened, the parents expressed their great delight, as this was progress – previously he would have fondled the TA's breasts without asking.

In another case, a pupil with ADHD was constantly interrupting the lesson and interfering with other pupils. Moving him to the front of the classroom on the left-hand side, made it more awkward for him to turn to face the class, as he was right-handed, so it was more obvious when he did move. In addition, when he did become restless, I would write down the time in his book, wherever he had got up to; a couple of minutes later I could wander past and see how much he had done since I had last been past! This helped to keep him on task at key points in the lesson.

These stories illustrate the need to pay particular attention to the needs of all pupils, and it may not be appropriate to see those needs as purely history specific.

Target setting is an important part of progressing. Targets for pupils will vary considerably. Some pupils may have an IEP that contains their particular targets, others may arise from pieces of work that have been done and may be short, medium or long term. But it is important to remember that all pupils have different needs and therefore need different targets. To accommodate this, some departments use a simple sheet stuck on the inside cover of exercise books to specify individual targets. Some could be general ones linked to literacy, behaviour or participation, while one could be subject specific, e.g:

1   I will always read through my work and ask a friend to read it to make sure it makes sense.

2   I will try to answer at least one question in every lesson.

3   I will think about the reasons for things happening. (As work progresses week by week, this particular target could change to reflect the nature of the work being undertaken.)

Partly to accommodate the needs of pupils with more severe difficulties, the QCA have recently devised P levels (see Figure 7.5 below for a breakdown of these), which allow targets to be set for pupils operating below National Curriculum levels. These allow for sensible targets to be set and progression to be made according to the needs of the individual child. The first three levels are generic to all subjects, but the levels after that are specific to subjects, and once attained lead into National Curriculum level 1.

The examples given are drawn from the KS 1 and 2 units of study that may be more appropriate for pupils with more severe learning difficulties. In particular, the emphasis on personal history provides the familiar starting point from which to extend pupils' understanding. The use of timelines can be an important way for pupils to grasp a sense of changes within their own lifetime, and highlight key moments and developments. Pictures or photos can be good visual prompts for such a task that can then be talked through and sequenced either from memory or clues within the pictures.

Once this has been acquired, the sense of time can be taken further back by producing timelines based on other members of the family. This can then provide opportunities to compare and contrast the experiences of different people at different times. This enables key historical ideas like chronology, change and continuity, and different characteristics of periods to be discussed.

In addition, alongside these family timelines, can be set momentous events that are local, national, or global, whichever is seem as more appropriate. This starts to provide a wider context to the pupil's own life. To emphasise the idea of change or difference between periods of time, sets of pictures can be discussed and sorted into categories, such as modern objects and objects before the pupil's lifetime. Working with artefacts can promote good quality thinking. Describing unusual objects is often the easy way into understanding their purpose, and revealing more about the time from which they came.

It may, however, be perfectly appropriate to use material from the key stage that is actually relevant to the age of the pupil. For example, in Year 9 it would be easy to allow pupils to engage with elements of the recent past. For example, it is possible to use video footage of the Blitz to create an understanding of the situation in London in the early years of the war. This could then be contrasted with local and personal history from the same period. By interviewing family members from the period and looking at sources linked to the locality, contrasts between the different experiences of war can be made, and the diversity of the past can be emphasised.

Pupils, however, could also work their way up the P levels through using local history that may well fit into other areas of study. Old photos from the 1900s can offer an insight into the past that can be contrasted with the current

P1 (i) *Pupils encounter activities and experiences. They may be passive or resistant. They may show simple reflex responses,* for example, startling at sudden noises or movements. *Any participation is fully prompted.*

P1 (ii) *Pupils show emerging awareness of activities and experiences. They may have periods when they appear alert and ready to focus their attention on certain people, events, objects or parts of objects,* for example, catching the smell of old fabric or wooden artefacts. *They may give intermittent reactions,* for example, sometimes becoming quiet or tense when going into an ancient building.

P2 (i) *Pupils begin to respond consistently to familiar people, events and objects. They react to new activities and experiences,* for example, looking to the source of unfamiliar sights and sounds in dramatisations of historical events. *They begin to show interest in people, events and objects,* for example, tracking historical artefacts into or out of their field of awareness. *They accept and engage in coactive exploration,* for example, touching wood, stone or old brick structures during site visits.

P2 (ii) *Pupils begin to be proactive in their interactions. They communicate consistent preferences and affective responses,* for example, wanting to look at a particular photograph. *They recognise familiar people, events and objects,* for example, smiling at an item from their own family home. *They perform actions, often by trial and improvement, and they remember learned responses over short periods of time,* for example, patting an old toy. *They co-operate with shared exploration and supported participation,* for example, when handling historical artefacts.

P3 (i) *Pupils begin to communicate intentionally. They seek attention through eye contact, gesture or action. They request events or activities,* for example, vocalising for more sound in a simulation of historical events. *They participate in shared activities with less support. They sustain concentration for short periods. They explore materials in increasingly complex ways,* for example, looking at, and touching, old objects. *They observe the results of their own actions with interest,* for example, when exploring an antique mechanical toy. *They remember learned responses over more extended periods,* for example, recalling gestures used in a dramatisation of a historical story from session to session.

P3 (ii) *Pupils use emerging conventional communication. They greet known people and may initiate interactions and activities,* for example, prompting an adult to look through a family album with them. *They can remember learned responses over increasing periods of time and may anticipate known events,* for example, becoming excited at a key moment in a video of a school trip or family holiday. *They may respond to options and choices with actions or gestures,* for example, eye-pointing to an old toy from their own past. *They actively explore objects and events for more extended periods,* for example, moving around a historical site. *They apply potential solutions systematically to problems,* for example, gesturing towards the location for a new activity at the end of a session. *(continues over)*

Figure 7.5 *P levels taken from www.nc.uk.net*

P4 *Pupils recognise themselves and other people in pictures of the recent past. They link the passage of time with a variety of indicators,* for example, weekend activities, summer holidays or seasonal changes. *They use single words, signs or symbols to confirm the function of everyday items from the past,* for example, 'cup', 'bed', 'house'.

P5 *Pupils know they took part in past events and they listen and respond to familiar stories about their own past. They begin to communicate about activities and events in the past,* for example, saying or signing 'baby toys', in response to personal items from their own early childhood. *With some prompting or support, they answer simple questions about historical artefacts and buildings,* for example, identifying a bowl as being made out of wood.

P6 *Pupils recognise and make comments about themselves and people they know in pictures of the more distant past. They recognise some obvious distinctions between the past and the present in their own lives and communicate about these,* for example, noting their attendance at a different school in the past. *They begin to pick historical artefacts out from collections of items,* for example, identifying old plates, items of clothing or hand tools.

P7 *Pupils begin to recognise some distinctions between the past and present in other people's lives as well as their own and communicate about these in simple phrases and statements. They listen to and follow stories about people and events in the past as well as events in their own lives. They sort objects to given criteria,* for example, old toys and new toys.

P8 *Pupils indicate if personal events and objects belong in the past or present. They begin to use some common words, signs or symbols to indicate the passage of time,* for example, now/then, today/yesterday. *They can recount episodes from their own past and some details from other historical events with prompts,* for example, past school or local events. *They answer simple questions about historical stories and artefacts.*

Figure 7.5 *continued*

locality – similarities and differences can be explored, and these can lead into more complex work on the reasons for change.

Even the more distant past can be made accessible. One of the key points is to start with the familiar and then work backwards. When looking at Tudor times, a pupil might be asked to describe a scene from their own street – what can they see, hear, smell. They could then be asked to consider which of the things they have mentioned might be the same in a Tudor street. After this initial speculation, using a range of sources, they could then be challenged to explain what they might be able to see, hear and smell in a Tudor street.

Examining the distant past might be made even more immediate. A pupil might be asked to describe their experience of childhood, what they played with, who they stayed with, what their family was like and so on. This could be compared directly with the experiences of children in Tudor times by asking such questions as: What toys did Tudor children play with? Who looked after them? Did they go to school? If not, what did they do? To make this task even more accessible, this could be translated into an exercise, in which pupils have to divide pictures into modern and Tudor scenes.

Alternative accreditation

Entry level certification exists within history. This is offered by all the exam boards, and is designed to cater for students who are generally operating at levels 2 or 3 of the National Curriculum, and thus may be appropriate for particular pupils.

This level of certification has a number of advantages. The course is similar in content to GCSE history courses, so students can work within a mixed-ability setting. The actual course content is greatly reduced, but has clear overlaps with all the main GCSE specifications.

Assessment is also very flexible and designed to meet the needs of the pupils. For example, the AQA specification offers five compulsory topics of which pupils do two. Two of the topics are based on medicine, two on the twentieth century and one on the Agricultural Revolution. For each topic there are three externally set assignments, but the pupils only have to do one on each of their compulsory topics. They could do all the assignments related to a topic and then pick the best for each topic, which gives greater chances for success. In addition, these externally set assignments can be done when the candidates are ready. The assignments are internally marked but externally moderated. The AQA course then offers 43 further units that can be done as optional studies, of which pupils need to do four. Any combination is possible, and each unit is self-contained and focuses on topics as diverse as disease from 1800 to the present day, the lifestyle of the Plains Indians and race and youth in Nazi Germany. Each unit that is tackled needs to show evidence of work done, but this is clearly detailed within the specification which outlines possible work that would be suitable. For example, on the unit about the changing nature of warfare, 'WWII to the Atomic bomb', students need to have demonstrated the ability to:

1   compare contemporary sources about the bombing of Dresden and Hiroshima to draw up a table of at least two differences between how the bombings were carried out and their effect on the war;

2   use eyewitness accounts of the bombing of Hiroshima to write a list of observations that people made to describe what happened during the atomic explosion;

3   identify from modern interpretations two reasons why some people now think it was a mistake to have dropped the Atom bomb on Hiroshima;

4   identify from modern interpretations two reasons why some people still think it was right to use the Atom bomb on Hiroshima;

shown knowledge of

5 two alternative courses of action that President Truman could have taken to end the war without dropping the Atom bomb in 1945;

6 at least three consequences of the use of the Atom bomb during the post war period;

experienced

7 contributing to an illustrated wall display, which might be used with Junior School children to inform them about Hiroshima.

(AQA website: www.aqa.org.uk)

In terms of assessment, the following would be needed:

A student's folder of work containing:

- student-produced table (1)

- student-completed worksheet(s) (2–6)

- Teacher-completed checklist (7)

For further information about these specifications go to the relevant examination board website.

A new idea currently under consideration at the time of writing is a completely new style GCSE being piloted by the QCA. A pilot is planned for September 2005. The 'hybrid' GCSE is designed to be accessible for all students and aims to broaden the appeal of history, and build on current good practice at KS3. It covers relatively new content areas and has a slightly different focus from current GCSE specifications.

The exam can be taken as a half or full GCSE. Within the half GCSE, pupils would study three core units:

- *Local history* – The focus will be on an investigation that should focus on the significance of an historical issue/site/event/development to the local community in the past, and to the students' own lives, their community and its future. This would be a practical based task.

- *National history* – This would focus on a period of time, in which the key idea would be to explore diversity of experience. This would allow stereotypical views of the past to be challenged, and the aim is to look at areas covered at KS3, but that are largely ignored at KS4 currently.

- *International history* – This would focus on a controversial topic in recent history and examine how different protagonists, the media and historians have portrayed the event. The aim is for pupils to see the relevance of history and how it can be used and abused.

The new exam is also planned to be more imaginative in assessment procedures. There would need to be some external assessment of the core units, but this may be as little as 50–60 per cent, thus giving greater emphasis to internal assessment. In terms of internal assessment, the intention is to build in more opportunities for oral assessment, presentations and portfolios of work. At the moment, if the full GCSE was taken, the idea is that the additional units would also be internally assessed. Further information can be obtained from the History Officer at QCA.

CHAPTER 8

Managing Support

The prerequisite to managing classroom support is to ensure that you are actually allocated some in the first place! In many schools, history departments are allocated only the remnants of support time once the demands of the core subjects have been attended to. It has to be recognised that the criteria usually used to classify a pupil as having a special need are often those of lack of proficiency in reading, writing and numerical skills. When such criteria are used to identify a special need and are established as priorities in the minds of parents well before secondary school, it is unlikely that a history department's requests for support will be given priority over those of the English and mathematics departments unless the head of history is very clear in his or her own mind both about how support will be used and of the particular benefits support in history lessons will bring to a child.

Such truisms, particularly the assumption that reading and writing can best be developed in the English classroom, can be challenged. Indeed logically, for focused *application and deployment* of English, history as a subject can help a pupil with special needs make astonishing progress. History can provide the concrete and contextual examples of usage of language *for a purpose*. This provides an essential complement to the English department's tuition of the structure of language and, as such, should be seen as an equal partner subject in helping a child with special educational needs develop proficiency and confidence in the use of language.

There is, then, no need to be defensive about the potential of history as a subject in its own right to build the skills and, just as importantly, the confidence of a child with special educational needs. When bidding for support, refer directly to the KSUs specified in 'History in the National Curriculum' (DfEE, QCA, 1999) and emphasise their relevance to *all* pupils, but – in this context of gaining classroom support time – particularly to pupils with SEN. For example:

- *Chronological understanding* – Provides a sense of relativity and sequence and gives a child a sense of his or her own context. This encourages focus on events outside of immediate personal experience while contextualising that personal experience. This potential for studies moving from the personal to the contextual is of great value, since personal experience is a powerful entry point to many concepts for pupils with a wide variety of learning difficulties. Study of chronology is particularly valuable for pupils with autism.

- *Knowledge and understanding of events, people and changes in the past* – Potential is high here for edging towards empathetic identification with people in the past – taking advantage of the requirement to study 'ideas, beliefs and attitudes of men, women and children in the past'. Whether empathy itself is ever fully attainable is a moot point, but the process of *striving* for empathy using textual, aural, visual and sensory sources (such as the smell and sheer weight of a steel helmet) will provide a bridge between a child's personal experiences and those of people in the past. Again, this is an accessible entry point leading to learning goals limited only by aspiration. History, of all subjects, lends itself superbly to access for all and to differentiation by outcome and, if the selected subject matter catches a child's imagination, that outcome can surprise pupil and teacher alike. If a child's attainment exceeds his or her previous expectation then confidence and self-belief will increase – and the extent to which these are present makes a huge difference to a child's learning potential. History, with its wealth of stimulus material, its diversity of sources, and its sheer breadth of human experience (with its associated treasure house of wonderful stories), has greater potential than most subjects to catch the imagination of a child – whatever that child's learning difficulties.

- *Historical Interpretations* – Easy to dismiss as 'too difficult' even for many mainstream pupils. Yet Christine Counsell has shown that with use of film sources, interpretations can be made accessible. Why was such a background chosen? How does this background music shape our idea of that character? Why is Cromwell shown alone in the opening sequence? Such study can move a child away from blind acceptance of things as they are towards the confidence and ability to challenge an accepted view – and even to form a view of his or her own – however simple that view might be.

- *Historical Enquiry* – To allow a child to find out for his or herself from a starting point of selected and adapted sources can produce a great sense of achievement – particularly in areas of enquiry where substantial doubt remains despite years of attention by professional historians: Who could Jack the Ripper have been? Was William Rufus' death in the New Forest an accident or murder? What happened to Amelia Earhart? Why was JFK killed? A child's hypothesis can be constructed from the discipline of source work and can stand alongside the hypotheses of university professors. Of course, appropriate sources will need to be adapted and provided to give that all-important accessibility. But, once this is done, the sense of reward and self-worth opened to pupils by successfully constructing an hypothesis is a prize worth having indeed. How many IEPs have you seen that place increase of self-esteem as a high priority target? Learning difficulty can so easily lower a pupil's sense of self-worth. Here is a way of actively boosting that sense.

- *Organisation and Communication* – As shown above, organisation and communication *for a purpose* provides incentive to organise and communicate as well as possible. The organisation and communication *does not have to be written*. The order clearly states that pupils should 'communicate their knowledge and understanding of history using a range of techniques including spoken language, structured narratives, substantiated explanations and the use of ICT.' Not only is the form highly flexible, but the degree of structure and the level of substantiation can vary widely too and can be assessed from use of the P scales or the appropriate statement of attainment from the NC Attainment Target. Many pupils working to an IEP will need to build communication and organisational skills.

Bidding for support

Such are the general opportunities and challenges history provides for pupils with SEN. These alone can boost a department's case when bidding for support, but it would be unwise in the extreme to depend only on the general case. The wise head of history should gain access to information about the particular special needs and existing IEPs of the incoming Year 7 as soon as possible. Do not wait for details to appear in your pigeon-hole three weeks or more into the new school year. See your SENCO on the Professional Development day at the start of the year or, better still, when the data is coming in towards the end of the previous school year. This will be useful for bidding for support on the basis of numbers of children with SEN, but will also provide details on the *specific needs* of each child. Then the KSUs of the NC in history can be matched to a child's specific requirements, and the department can make an effective case for support with a clear knowledge of how support will be used. In short, history can be mentioned specifically in the new IEP as it is constructed. A SENCO will be grateful for such involvement and the resultant specific, measurable, achievable, relevant (SMART) targets which will result:

- A child with low self-esteem, for example, could be allocated support with specific reference to the building of personal hypotheses based on evidence.

- A child with communication difficulties could be encouraged to use ICT and supported in that use.

- A kinaesthetic learner with ADHD could be supported in the role play and practical demonstration activities so essential for his or her effective learning – yet so full of potential for over-excitement.

Once support time has been allocated to history, the HoD should not then back off allowing the SENCO to decide alone precisely where scarce support should be allocated during periods when several classes are studying history. A continuing dialogue should take place on the best allocation of support. Of course, decisions should be made primarily on the basis of the number of pupils with special needs and the severity of those special needs in any class and, of course, support is often allocated to a particular pupil allowing little flexibility – but where some flexibility does exist, these factors should be at least considered in making a decision:

- *What is the broader picture within a particular class?* A child with relatively mild special needs may be badly neglected if a teacher is preoccupied with several disruptive or particularly demanding pupils. Conversely, a child with severe special needs may make significant progress in a class where the learning atmosphere is good.

- *What is the real attitude of the class teacher towards pupils with special needs?* Meeting the needs of mainstream pupils in a class can be a daunting task in itself and a significant number of pupils with special needs may just be too much for some individuals to cope with. Will support focus such a teacher on his or her SEN pupils – or will support be wasted or diverted to trivial classroom tasks? Here, if support is not flexible, then the HoD can use his or her powers to switch departmental staff with reference to the number of SEN pupils in a class. INSET on the use of in-class support may remove the issue.

- *How well do departmental staff work with an extra adult in the classroom?* Will staff feel self-conscious or be genuinely unaware of how support should be used? Have staff had sufficient INSET on use of in-class support?

- *Is a member of staff working in a specific history classroom – perhaps his or her own?* A teacher allocated a classroom not normally used for the teaching of history – and therefore devoid of a ready-to-hand supply of texts and other basic equipment may well find it more difficult to address pupils' special educational needs than would otherwise be the case. Both pupils and teacher in such a situation may benefit from allocation of additional support.

How will support be used?

Once support has been allocated, the process of forming a triangular learning team needs to commence:

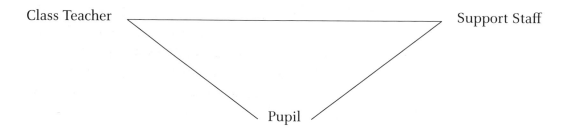

Be in no doubt that support staff and teachers must see themselves as part of a team if subject learning objectives and IEP targets are to be achieved. There should be department input into LSA training days, and most certainly support staff should be included in at least some departmental meetings. The biggest obstacle to effective use of support staff is lack of communication between them and the class teacher. The nightmare scenario is one where the class teacher keeps his or her short-term planning a closely guarded secret from support staff. This leads to a situation whereby the support member of staff is forced to absorb the content, concepts and skills of the lesson and almost simultaneously adopt differentiation strategies to make these accessible to pupils who will almost certainly have a wide variety of differing learning difficulties or needs. All that can ever come of such an approach is frustration: frustration for the pupils who are on the receiving end of hastily adopted teaching strategies; frustration for support staff who never get a chance to think through how best to address learning objectives which may well not be clear to them – even in the unlikely event that they are subject specialists – in such limited absorption time; and ultimately great frustration for the class teacher who will certainly find himself explaining to support staff for a second or third time, as well as trying to field questions from pupils, with or without special needs!

Such a situation of hand-to-mouth SEN provision can easily arise in the frantic hustle and bustle of today's secondary schools. Teachers will *mean* to plan lessons early; will *mean* to consult IEPs about individual pupil targets; will *mean* to at least consult, and possibly even involve, support staff within the short-term planning process. In practice, however, with as many as fifteen history classes to teach with the associated heavy marking load inherent to this subject (possibly above all others), content rich and constantly changing GCSE and A level specifications to absorb and adapt, duties to do between lessons, pastoral incidents, physical movement around very large buildings and a demanding meeting load after school, it is all too easy for a class teacher to have no contact at all with support staff from one lesson to the next. Teachers know much of what *should* be done to help pupils with special needs and frequently carry guilt complexes concerning this – but how often is true integrated planning involving support staff actually done on a regular basis without the dreadful incentive of an impending visit from Ofsted? Any advice given below is offered in the spirit of the desirable, the aspirational – but also the workable – since, without the latter, we just give teachers a model for the Ofsted week and further fuel for guilt for the rest of the time.

Points for planning and feedback

- In the majority of situations, support staff will not be subject specialists. They will, therefore need, specific guidance through existing departmental plans of the historical KSUs, forming the basis of the learning objectives for the lesson. After all, this is a *history* lesson and, if pupils (with or without special educational needs) do not leave the room without their knowledge skills or understanding of that subject enhanced, then the lesson will not have been satisfactory. In practice, support staff will need a copy of the departmental medium-term plan upon which should be found:

- a lesson sequence for the term;
- learning objectives with reference to the KSUs of the National Curriculum in history;
- an outline of learning activities;
- available resources;
- expected learning outcomes for the majority of pupils.

In addition, they should be encouraged to read the KSUs and the level statements themselves to gain at least an outline idea of the content and progression set out therein. This will at least give a context for the learning of the pupils being supported. It is essential that the class teacher takes responsibility here for making the support teacher comfortable with the historical material being covered. For some support staff it will be possible to discuss the medium-term plan in half-termly chunks (see Figure 8.1 for an example); for others, monthly meetings will be required. Obviously the more time for quality discussion the better and a weekly meeting would be ideal but, in practice, this may not be possible. The vital thing is that class and support staff get time to establish a dialogue about the *history* being taught – through this, the support staff will gain a working knowledge of the teacher's style and approach and the teacher will gain a feel of the subject confidence of the support teacher:

Practical demonstration card

The power of the machine gun

Purpose

To reinforce in the pupils' minds the relative power of the machine gun when compared to previously available weapons.

Method

1. Ask a pupil with a watch registering seconds to act as timekeeper.

2. Simulate with the class the firing of a bolt-action rifle. Bang! Click . . . Click . . . bang! Ask timekeeper how long it took from one bang to the next. (Should be approximately ten seconds.)

3. Explain that a machine gun fired 300 rounds per minute in 1914. This meant five rounds per second.

4. Tap on the desk with a board writer at the pace of five rounds per second.

5. Repeat drill with bolt action rifle. Discuss difference in rate of fire. What effect would machine-gun fire have on men moving across open ground?

(Please see Figure 8.1 for context.)

- Support staff will bring experience of supporting pupils with a wide variety of special needs. They may well have been instrumental in drawing up IEPs for pupils in a particular class and will probably have experience of the individual personalities of those pupils from supporting them lower down in the school

KSU Learning Intentions	Enquiry Questions	Learning Activities	Resources	Teaching Monitoring of Learning Outcomes
Pupils will be able to: use techniques of WW1 propaganda to design a recruiting poster.	Why did so many volunteer to join the army?	• Examination of concept of 'motivation'. Mystery 'Why did Oliver Hopkin join the army? N.B. OLIVER HOPKIN WAS FROM SUFFOLK *NOT* DURHAM. Is it legitimate to change a source in this way? Discuss. • Study a selection of recruiting posters. What methods do they use to encourage enlistment? Design a poster to encourage recruits, using one of the techniques identified. • Was conscription justified?	*Thinking Through History* Peter Fisher, Chris Kington publications. Posters available from Imperial War Museum on postcards.	Can pupils explain a variety of motivations for enlistment?
Know about a wider range of sources of information	What did soldiers experience in the trenches of the Great War?	• Using the practical demonstration card, explain and demonstrate the effectiveness of a machine gun against advancing troops. Ask pupils to explain why trenches were dug!	PRACTICAL DEMONSTRATION CARD 2 'THE MACHINE GUN' (see above)	
Begin to recognise uses and limitations of different types of evidence.		• Look at the drawings of trench conditions in Byrom and Shephard. Compare with a selection of photographs. Discuss the advantages/disadvantages of both mediums. • Move to written sources such as Gurney's letter (Byrom p.15) or the accounts of troops on Shephard p.14–15. How much do these add? Move on to, poetry, prose and clips from feature films such as *The Trench*, or the later re-make of *All Quiet on the Western Front* (1979)	OHTs of trench conditions Byrom p.15 Shephard p.14–15 *All Quiet on the Western Front* Erich Maria Remarque ISBN 009953281	Can pupils describe life in the trenches, using a wide range of information sources?
Describe and exemplify key features of past situations.		• Extended writing. Write a letter home from the trenches Explain to those at home the conditions under which you are living, making use of the mediums studied to make your account as accurate as possible.	*Testament of Youth* Vera Brittain	

Figure 8.1 Medium-term planning

(or from liaison with primary school staff in the case of Year 7). They often will have supported the same child in several subject areas and will, therefore, have a strong appreciation of that child's strengths and weaknesses across much of the wider curriculum. It is this expertise that provides the support staff's contribution to the three-way team referred to above. It is an invaluable contribution and must be seen as such by the class teacher. It is often a failure to appreciate this that leads to underestimation of the potential of support staff. The art is how to tap this experience for the benefit of the pupils and the spile for this tap must be one of short-term planning.

- Short-term planning *must* provide a synthesis whereby the history learning objectives of the lesson meet the special needs of the individual child through addressing the IEP specified targets. A planning sheet such as that provided by Anne Watkinson in *The Essential Guide for Experienced Teaching Assistants* does provide a vehicle for consideration of both historical learning objectives and the individual needs of the child. Some problems (though not insurmountable ones) do arise from the use of such a sheet. An example of such a planning sheet and of a teacher's generic whole-class plan is in Figure 8.2. Who should fill the sheet in? Is it the TA's responsibility after having seen the teachers 'whole-class' plan? This would allow flexibility for the support staff and would provide an opportunity to apply individual knowledge of the child with an holistic view of the historical learning objectives and perceived flow of the lesson. On the other hand, this approach allows no opportunity for the support staff to warn of impossible activities with a particular child, or to make suggestions as to what will be particularly effective, given knowledge of a pupil's particular strengths or preferred learning style.

  Or is it the teacher's responsibility, at least initially, to attempt to provide accessibility to the whole-class plan by at least starting to fill in a planning sheet for each pupil with an IEP? This involves the class teacher to the full and is a reminder that pupils with special needs are not some kind of annexe to the class but are a part of it with full rights. Yet, is it realistic to expect a teacher to suggest differentiated activities for what may be as many as ten or more pupils with IEPs? Clearly, if planning were done jointly and simultaneously by class teacher and support staff, this would maximise learning opportunities in history for all pupils. If arrangements can be made to work such an approach nothing else will come close – but teachers and support staff do need to go home occasionally, and non-contact periods are not always conveniently situated – or even in existence – given cover demands in some schools.

The best compromise would seem to be for the teacher to fill in the generic class plan prioritising history learning objectives and expected learning outcomes, thus maximising the chance to think deeply about his or her true area of expertise. This would then be given to the support staff, via pigeon hole if necessary, *sufficiently in advance of the lesson* to allow the TA to apply knowledge and experience of individual needs in drawing up differentiated approaches on a form similar or identical to Anne Watkinson's (see Figure 8.2).

One 90 minute lesson or two 50 minute ones

Learning Objective

KSU 2 'Knowledge and understanding of events, people and attitudes in the past'. Specific reference to 2a 'attitudes of men, women and children in the past', in an exploration of attitudes to recruitment in WW1.

Enquiry question: Why did people volunteer for the armed forces in WW1?

Starter Phase

1. Class idea session to introduce the concept of motives. What *makes* people do anything? Use examples of: homework; chores; exercise; burglaries; leave home; fight; get married. Initially look for any motive. Pupils to list motives for each then pool ideas in a whole-class discussion session.

2. Move on to discuss idea of push/pull factors influencing any decision, e.g. *Marriage*: Pull factor = love. Push factor = wish to leave home.

Main Teaching Phase

1. Form pupils into discussion groups of three. Use the cards from Fisher *Thinking Skills in History* on push pull factors influencing Oliver Parkin's decision to join the army. Pupils to group cards into push/pull factors.

2. Move on to look at push factors and pull factors that were particular only to Parkin, then ones that could be generally applied. Pupils, still in groups, rank these new groups of factors as to importance. How high has each group placed recruitment posters (mentioned on one card)?

3. Explain that you are now going to test their theories by examining this means of encouraging recruitment since it embodied both push and pull factors.

4. Pass round numbered posters asking groups to record for each the methods employed to encourage recruitment, e.g. shame; sexual attraction; fear, etc.

5. Look at extract from film *Oh what a Lovely War, Gallipoli* or *All Quiet on the Western Front*. Explore hero's motive for joining in each case.

Plenary Phase

1. Discussion and learning review: What have we seen that would be effective in boosting army recruitment? Why would those techniques have been successful?

2. In groups again, with the task of designing a publicity campaign to boost recruitment for the First World War. Groups may use any techniques discussed plus original ideas such as songs, poems or flags to present to the rest of the group. Homework plus first 15 minutes of next lesson to prepare presentations.

Figure 8.2 *Exemplar plan by class teacher*

Support staff action sheet

Date: 32/13/2004   Teacher: Mr Luff

TA: Mr Smith

Class: Year 9 mixed ability. 28 pupils. 4 on IEPs.

Learning objective(s) KSU 2 'Knowledge and understanding of events, people and attitudes in the past'. Specific reference to 2a 'attitudes of men, women and children in the past', in an exploration of attitudes to recruitment in WW1.

Enquiry question: Why did people volunteer for the armed forces in WW1?

Learning outcomes Can pupils explain a variety of motivations for enlistment?

TA Activities

Starter

Circulate amongst SEN children. Build confidence by praising ideas on motives. Help record in rough list for dyslexic pupils. Talk one to one with autistic pupils.

Main Input Phase

Groups will have been pre-chosen to provide maximum inclusion of pupils with SEN. Circulate among groups, sit alongside mainstream and SEN pupils to remove stigma. Carefully observe pupils with SEN to intervene early in case of real difficulty/loss of concentration – particularly for ADHD pupil. Help interpret cards for dyslexic pupils.

Circulate among pupils to 'tease out' ideas from video. Sit close to ADHD pupil when video is on.

Plenary/Learning Review Phase

Arrange for class teacher to look for contributions from pupils with SEN in plenary phase. Position close to pupils who may struggle – point to recorded ideas as prompted. Work with groups as above. Use SEN homework club to support individual ideas of pupils with SEN.

Resources

Thinking skills in History Peter Fisher. Card sets. Video clips (see main plan)

IEP input

Children	Steven	Adrian	Cynthia	Ravinder
Individual needs	ADHD. Mild dyslexia. Can disrupt when frustrated. **IEP focus:** improve concentration.	Severe dyslexia. Finds both reading and writing very difficult. **IEP focus:** build up confidence in these areas	Dyslexic. Low self-esteem. Can withdraw if given too much challenge too quickly. **IEP focus:** build pride in work.	Autistic. Not disruptive but very reluctant to engage in whole-class discussion. **IEP focus:** encourage oral contribution.
Feedback comments				

Form adapted from Anne Watkinson's *The Essential Guide for Experienced Teaching Assistants*

Figure 8.2 *continued*

Ideally these approaches would be shown to the class teacher and discussed before the lesson takes place – but constraints of timetable or building may prevent this. A dialogue at this short-term planning stage will always pay off if one can be arranged. Five minutes at break time before the lesson is better than nothing – and certainly better than expectations of long, involved discussions which will not take place. As long as an extensive dialogue has occurred around the medium-term plan then long discussions at the short-term stage are not essential. Please see 'points for planning and feedback' earlier in this chapter.

The bottom line is that planning should allow learning objectives in history to be synthesised with IEP targets and addressed through accessible learning activities. If this is happening, then however the process is being facilitated fades into the background. Aim for the ideal of frequent and regular dialogue but do not flagellate yourself should the ideal not prove possible *as long as joint address by class teacher and support staff of pupil learning opportunities is being prioritised.*

- The pupil also must not be neglected as a member of the learning team. His or her reaction to learning activities and progress towards expected learning outcomes must be taken into account through some form of feedback system. Again Anne Watkinson's planning sheet (Figure 8.2) provides a valuable opportunity for feedback. Successful approaches are documented as such, and failures will be evident. In practice, the most viable way to record successes and failures in the long term could well be to annotate the medium-term plan (see Figure 8.1) in pencil or attached Post-its: 'Unsuitable for severely autistic pupils'; 'Particularly helpful for dyslexic pupils'; 'Try this to gain the attention of ADHD pupils . . .' At the end of the year, such comments could be amalgamated into the medium-term plan permanently in a meeting involving history department staff, support staff and the Head of history. Dialogue here will be invaluable for raising awareness of special needs issues.

- Lack of specialist support staff need not be an issue with planning. In many ways, support from a non-history teacher can provide a refreshing new look at approaches to facilitating understanding, can anticipate pupil questions and can be a useful challenge to assumptions of knowledge. How often have we as history teachers plunged into technical terms without thinking that such terms and the concepts they address may not be common knowledge after all? What, for example, is the difference between a bomb and a shell? Why was a round keep so much stronger than a square one? If specialist support is available count your lucky stars – then you have available a person with historical skills and specialist knowledge of special needs. Try not to feel threatened: how much richer will be the dialogues about learning objectives and IEPs now!

Support in the classroom environment

Now we have planned as a team it is essential to put that plan into practice as a team also. While the lesson is going on, class teacher and support staff must work in harmony to previously agreed rules, designed to avert common causes of friction.

1 *Will the support teacher talk while the teacher is talking to the rest of the class?*

   This presents both support teacher and class teacher with a dilemma. The class teacher will want silence when he or she is presenting from the front of the room and will have insisted on full attention from the class. In this situation, the 'magic' can easily be broken by a murmur as the support teacher explains or elaborates on a point for a pupil. Once the 'magic' is broken then other pupils will take advantage by breaking into their own private conversations and the atmosphere of concentration will quickly be lost. Conversely, if total silence from support staff and pupils alike is insisted upon, then the support teacher finds him or herself having to sit back, even when the pupil being supported is clearly having difficulty. By the very nature of history, teacher talk will extend beyond mere 'instruction giving': it will be used to create atmosphere, to interpret a text, and to establish context. The best compromise will probably be for the support teacher to take notes on teacher input for explanation at a later stage of the lesson. For this to work, class teacher input must be split into manageable chunks and the pupil being supported must be told that he or she is not being ignored but that support will be available during an appropriate moment. Many pupils will accept this and even feel grateful to be spared the embarrassment of being singled out to be spoken to, when all the other pupils are expected to listen to the class teacher.

   If a pupil's needs are such that he or she cannot wait even for a short period of time, then the class needs to be told that all must stay silent but Mrs X may need to talk on occasions. On no account should the supported pupil's name be broadcast. The key point is that an agreement must be made and adhered to by both class teacher and support staff.

2 *Who responds to questions from supported pupils?*

   Often if the class teacher responds, the support teacher can easily be labelled 'not a proper teacher' in the eyes of all the pupils in the room. This carries a penalty in the shape of loss of authority and of dignity. Yet, if the class teacher never comes near nor by, the sense of inclusion of the supported pupil can be severely damaged. Both staff should be involved. Again a simple, clear agreement should be entered into – perhaps on the basis of physical proximity. The pupil simply asks the closest member of staff. If the support teacher cannot answer a technical historical question, then the class teacher can be called by both support teacher and supported pupil. This will have only a temporary effect on the support teacher's standing since he or she will be able to answer many questions (owing, at least partly, to the planning process described above), but will also boost the self-esteem of a supported pupil since an adult didn't know the answer either.

3   *Should a support teacher remain next to a pupil being supported for the whole lesson?*
    Manifestly, no. All pupils need the chance to strike out alone at times. A sense of independence must be fostered and the sensitivity of a pupil who is reaching the highly sensitive stage of puberty must be respected. Boys in particular can react in an extreme manner to over-intense support. Support staff can wander and should respond to questions from all pupils, thereby reducing the label of only being there for those who struggle.

4   *Who is responsible for the discipline in the room?*
    The responsibility clearly rests with the class teacher, but it should be made clear that instructions from support staff should be respected and obeyed. The vital point is that class teacher and support staff should discuss and negotiate regarding strategies for response to possible discipline issues. These frequently can be anticipated and, of course, avoided, as familiarity with pupils increases and is taken into account when planning. As a general rule of thumb, the class teacher should handle whole-class addresses such as 'that noise level does not allow concentration', whereas the nearest teacher can respond to individual or localised bad behaviour.

5   *How much input should support staff give to individual pupil's work?*
    The question can arise as to whose work the finished piece actually is, particularly when an assessment is intended. Level of input should be as much as is necessary to allow the pupil a sense of achievement *providing:*

    - the class teacher is aware of how much help has been given;
    - such support reduces in subsequent pieces of similar work;
    - significant thinking input from the child, concordant with ability, has taken place.

    One useful way forward is for a TA to annotate a piece of work, explaining his or her input. In this way, both pupil and class teacher will get a realistic sense of the progress that has actually been made and the essential team work required between teacher, TA and the child.
    As referred to in Chapter 4, 'Teaching and Learning', a TA working with a child to check the process by which an answer has been reached, can be invaluable: not only in reinforcing learning, but also in strengthening the relationship between TA and pupil. This routine of the TA helping to review the methods by which learning has taken place makes it clear to the child that progress has been made through a *combination* of his or her own efforts and TA input. This can be a vital step in encouraging the child to work co-operatively with the TA in future lessons.

6   *Should support staff take part in role play and active learning?*
    Yes! Involvement on a regular basis will allow seamless intervention when

needed. Sitting out will only make intervention when required more obvious and more embarrassing to support teacher and pupil alike.

The key then to successful use of in-class support are the principles of mutual respect, open access to detailed medium-term planning, and involvement in short-term planning to synthesise IEP and history learning objectives. These principles will underlie clearly agreed rules as to the role of both class and support teacher when the lesson is actually in progress.

Appendices

Appendices

What do we really think?

Each member of the department should choose two of these statements and pin them on to the noticeboard for an overview of staff opinion. The person leading the session (Head of Department, SENCO, senior manager) should be ready to address any negative feedback and take forward the department in a positive approach.

If my own child had special needs, I would want her/him to be in a mainstream school mixing with all sorts of kids.

I want to be able to cater for pupils with SEN but feel that I don't have the expertise required.

Special needs kids in mainstream schools are all right up to a point, but I didn't sign up for dealing with the more severe problems – they should be in special schools.

It is the SENCO's responsibility to look out for these pupils with SEN – with help from support teachers.

Pupils with special needs should be catered for the same as any others. Teachers can't pick and choose the pupils they want to teach.

I need much more time to plan if pupils with SEN are going to be coming to my lessons.

Big schools are just not the right places for blind or deaf kids, or those in wheelchairs.

I would welcome more training on how to provide for pupils with SEN in history.

I have enough to do without worrying about kids who can't read or write.

If their behaviour distracts other pupils in any way, youngsters with SEN should be withdrawn from the class.

This is a photocopiable exercise.

SEN and Disability Act 2001 (SENDA)

1 The SEN and Disability Act 2001 amends the Disability Discrimination Act 1995 to include schools' and LEAs' responsibility to provide for pupils and students with disabilities.

2 The definition of a disability in this Act is:
'someone who has a physical or mental impairment that has an effect on his or her ability to carry out normal day to day activities. The effect must be:
- substantial (that is more than minor or trivial): and
- long term (that is, has lasted or is likely to last for at least a year or for the rest of the life of the person affected): and
- adverse.'

Activity: List any pupils that you come across that would fall into this category.

3 The Act states that the responsible body for a school must take such steps as it is reasonable to take to ensure that disabled pupils and disabled prospective pupils are not placed at substantial disadvantage in comparison with those who are not disabled.

Activity: Give an example of something which might be considered 'a substantial disadvantage'.

4 The duty on the school is to make reasonable adjustments is anticipatory. This means that a school should not wait until a disabled pupil seeks admission to consider what adjustments it might make generally to meet the needs of disabled pupils.

Activity: Think of two reasonable adjustments that could be made in your school/department.

5 The school has a duty to plan strategically for increasing access to the school education, this includes provision of information for pupils and parents (e.g. Braille or taped versions of brochures) improving the physical environment for disabled students and increasing access to the curriculum by further differentiation.

Activity: Consider ways of increasing access to the school for a pupil requesting admission who has Down's Syndrome with low levels of literacy and a heart condition that affects strenuous physical activity.

6 Schools need to be proactive in seeking out information about a pupil's disability (by establishing good relationships with parents and carers, asking about disabilities during admission interviews, etc.) and ensuring that all staff who might come across the pupil are aware of the pupil's disability.

Activity: List the opportunities that occur in your school for staff to gain information about disabled students. How can these be improved on?

Keeping strategies in mind

Special Educational Need	Characteristics	Strategies
Attention Deficit Disorder – with or without hyperactivity	• has difficulty following instructions and completing tasks • easily distracted by noise, movement of others, objects attracting attention • can't stop talking, interrupts others, calls out • acts impulsively without thinking about the consequences	• keep instructions simple – the one sentence rule • make eye contact and use the pupil's name when speaking to him • sit the pupil away from obvious distractions • provide clear routines and rules, rehearse them regularly
Autistic Spectrum Disorder	• may experience high levels of stress and anxiety when routines are changed • may have a literal understanding of language • more often interested in objects rather than people • may be sensitive to light, sound, touch or smell	• give a timetable for each day • warn the pupil about changes to usual routine • avoid using too much eye contact as it can cause distress • use simple clear language avoid using metaphor, sarcasm
Down's Syndrome	• takes longer to learn and consolidate new skills • limited concentration • has difficulties with thinking, reasoning, sequencing • has better social than academic skills • may have some sight, hearing, respiratory and heart problems	• use simple, familiar language • give time for information to be processed • break lesson up into a series of shorter, varied tasks • accept a variety of ways of recording work, drawings, diagrams, photos, video

Hearing Impairment	• may be mild, moderate or severe • may be monoaural, conductive, sensory or mixed loss	• check on the best seating position • check that the pupil can see your face for expressions and lip reading • indicate where a pupil is speaking from during class discussion, only allow one speaker at a time
Dyscalculia	• has a discrepancy between development level and general ability in maths • has difficulty counting by rote • misses out or reverses numbers • has difficulty with directions, left and right • losing track of turns in games, dance	• provide visual aids, number lines, lists of rules, formulae, words • encourage working out on paper • provide practical objects to aid learning

Instructions for activity

This activity should only take about ten minutes but can be used for additional discussion on strategies, concentrating on the easy ones to implement or the ones already being used.

1 Photocopy onto paper or card
2 Cut the first column off the sheet
3 Cut out the remaining boxes
4 Either keep the two sets of boxes separate, first matching the characteristics then the strategies, or use all together

Alternative activity: make the boxes bigger with room for additional strategies, or remove a couple of the strategies so staff can add any they have used or can identify.

References

Bakalis, M. (2003) 'Direct teaching of paragraph cohesion', *Teaching History,* **110**, 18–26. London: Historical Association.

Banham, D. (1998) 'Getting ready for the Grand Prix: learning how to build a substantiated argument in Year 7', *Teaching History,* **92**, 6–15.

Bruner, J. S. (1977) *The Process of Education,* Cambridge (Mass.). London: Harvard University Press.

Counsell, C. (2003) 'Fulfilling history's potential: nurturing tradition and renewal in a subject community', in Riley, M. and Harris, R. (eds) *Past Forward: A Vision for School History 2002–2012.* London: Historical Association, 6–11.

Curriculum Council for Wales (1991) Teacher Support Programme: Teaching History to Pupils with Severe and Moderate Learning Difficulties. Cardiff.

Detheridge, M. and Detheridge, T. (2002) *Literacy Through Symbols.* London: David Fulton Publishers.

DfES (2002) *Key Stage 3 National Strategy: Literacy in history.* London: DfES.

Fisher, P. (1999) 'Analysing Anne Frank: a case study in the teaching of thinking skills', *Teaching History,* **95**, 24–31. London: Historical Association.

Hammond, K. (2002) 'Getting Year 10 to understand the value of precise factual knowledge', *Teaching History,* **109**, 10–15. London: Historical Association.

Hughes, M. (1999) *Closing the Learning Gap.* Stafford: Network Educational Press.

Husbands, C. (1996) *What is History Teaching?* Buckingham: Open University Press.

Luff, I. (2000) '"I've been in the Reichstag". Rethinking Roleplay', *Teaching History,* **100**, 8–17. London: Historical Association.

Luff, I. (2001) 'Beyond "I speak, you listen, boy!" Exploring diversity of attitudes and experiences through speaking and listening', *Teaching History,* **105**, 10–17. London: Historical Association.

Luff, I. (2003) 'Stretching the strait jacket of assessment: use of Role Play and Practical Demonstration to enrich pupils' experience at GCSE and beyond', *Teaching History,* **113**, 26–35. London: Historical Association.

MacAleavy, T. (1994) 'Meeting pupils' learning needs: differentiation and progression in the teaching of history', in Bourdillon, H. (ed.) *Teaching History.* London and New York: Routledge, 153–168.

Martin, C. and Gummett, B. (2001) 'History' in Carpenter, B. *et al.* (eds) *Enabling Access* (2nd edn). London: David Fulton Publishers.

Martin, D. and Brooke, B. (2002) 'Getting personal: making effective use of historical fiction in the history classroom', *Teaching History* **108**, 30–35. London: Historical Association.

Moss, P. (1977 2nd edn.) *History Alive: 1900–70s.* St Albans: Hart-Davis Educational.

Mulholland, M. (1998) 'The evidence sandwich', *Teaching History*, **91**, 17–19

Phillips, R. (2001) 'Making history curious: Using Initial Stimulus Material (ISM) to promote enquiry, thinking and literacy', *Teaching History* **105**, 19–24. London: Historical Association.

Phillips, R. (2002) *Reflective Teaching of History 11–18*, London and New York: Continuum.

Piaget, Jean (1978) *The Development of Thought – equilibration of cognitive structures*. Translated from the French by Arnold Rosin. Oxford: Blackwell.

QCA, DfEE (1999) *History in the National Curriculum*. London: HMSO.

QCA (2000) *History: A scheme of work for key stage 3*. London: QCA.

Rathbone, J. (1998) *The Last English King*. London: Abacus.

Stakes, R. and Hornby, G. (2000) *Meeting Special Needs in Mainstream Schools: A Practical Guide for Teachers*. London: David Fulton Publishers.